A
CHANGE
OF HEART

Also by Julia Thorne

You Are Not Alone: Words of Experience
and Hope for the Journey Through Depression

A CHANGE OF HEART

WORDS OF EXPERIENCE AND HOPE
FOR THE JOURNEY THROUGH DIVORCE

JULIA THORNE

HarperPerennial
A Division of HarperCollinsPublishers

For Alexandra and Vanessa

HarperCollins books may be purchased for educational, business, or sales promotional use. For information please write: Special Markets Department, HarperCollins Publishers, Inc., 10 East 53rd Street, New York, NY 10022.

FIRST EDITION

Designed by Caitlin Daniels

Library of Congress Cataloging-in-Publication Data

Thorne, Julia, 1944–
    A change of heart : words of experience and hope for the journey through divorce / Julia Thorne. — 1st ed.
      p.   cm.
   ISBN 0–06–095105–2
    1. Divorce—United States—Psychological aspects. 2. Divorced people—United States—Case studies.   I. Title.
HQ814.T47   1996
306.89—dc20   95-53685

96 97 98 99 00 ❖/RRD 10 9 8 7 6 5 4 3 2 1

CONTENTS

INTRODUCTION

Shortly before I finished writing this book, I was told that a lawyer who worked as a guardian ad litem—a court-appointed children's advocate in contested custody cases—wanted to meet with me. She had heard that I was an "advocate for divorce," and she was worried. She thought I might need "a little education on how divorce affects children." In the meantime, she warned at least one school counseling office that I might be a risk. She suggested that allowing me to interview children whose parents were going through divorce was probably not a responsible thing to do.

I wanted to talk to her, too. I felt that I knew about divorce: after all, I was divorced, I was the child of divorce, and I was writing a book about divorce. I wanted to show her that I was not a risk so that I could continue my interviews with children attending local public schools.

When we met for lunch, I was expecting to see a stern and disapproving authority figure; instead, I found myself seated across from a sympathetic, intelligent, divorced and remarried mother of a four-year-old daughter. Before I could say anything, she smiled and explained that she had tracked down a friend of mine, a teacher in the school system, and had asked her about my character, history, and attitude toward divorce. Then she said, "I thought you were suggesting that everyone should get divorced. Now I know that you are recommending we support and empathize with individuals who are going through divorce. In fact, I guess it would be fair to say that you are an advocate for the adults going through divorce just as I am for the children who are caught in the process."

Pleasantly surprised, I admitted my own preconceptions about her. We laughed, and then proceeded to have a productive conversation about managing the divorce process. Once again, as had happened so often during my fourteen months of crisscrossing the country, interviewing individuals about their experiences with divorce, I had met another thoughtful professional who was quietly doing her best to improve the experience.

MAJOR LIFE TRANSITION

Divorce hurts. Divorce is a major life transition that reshapes our emotional identity and expectations and our sense of safety. All major life transitions—including birth, the death of a loved one, marriage, and life-threatening illness—involve varying degrees of pain and loss. With care and support, most of us are able over time to heal the wounds that accompany these transitions.

The wounds caused by divorce will heal, too. But the individuals and families struggling through its challenges may not receive the same care and support that are offered those suffering from some other form of trauma. Even though one out of every two American marriages now ends in divorce, our culture continues to judge the experience and shame the participants. Why do we so often withhold compassion from those suffering the traumas of this major life transition?

SILENT DISCRIMINATION

A friend of mine suggests that "divorce may be a last bastion of silent discrimination" in our culture. In fact, there are several ways in which we tend to punish people who divorce.

As a culture we are apt to discriminate against singles. Being single—especially a divorced single—is often considered a liability. Divorced men are suspected of being uncaring or withholding; some people assume that as husbands, these men were poor lovers or wife abusers. Divorced women may be considered "free radicals," a potential threat, untrustworthy, nagging, or neurotic. When you are part of a couple, it is assumed that you are healthier, happier, and more successful than a single person. In a conflict, the benefit of the doubt is tacitly given to the couple at the expense of the single. Culturally more powerful, a couple is invited to social occasions more often than a divorced single. Even the government discriminates, offering greater tax protection to married couples than to single people.

Single-parent families are considered inferior, too. The children of couples are thought to be more stable than children from divorced households, who are often pitied. Constance Ahrons, in her groundbreaking and hopeful book *The Good Divorce,* advises, "To recognize families of divorce as legitimate, we first have to shatter a deeply ingrained myth—the myth that only in a nuclear family can we raise healthy children."

The words that we use to describe divorce are another aspect of this silent discrimination, for they associate it with inadequacy and shame. We say, for example, that divorce results from a marriage that has "failed"; the couple has "split"; the children live in "broken homes."

The media usually portray divorce as a form of Armageddon, involving a fierce battle over who gets the house and/or the bank account—or worse yet, if the kids are reduced to "property," over who gets the kids. Individuals who choose to divorce are assumed to have character flaws. The media simplify and sensationalize divorce proceedings, characterizing them as confrontations based on greed or shallow stereotypes. Such portrayals only serve to polarize the people going through the divorce at a time when they most need support.

The media's superficial distortions, along with our national tendency to discriminate against those involved in divorce, have tragic results, including the emotional isolation of divorcing or divorced adults and the victimization of their children. By disregarding the true nature of divorce and by shaming divorced or divorcing individuals, we abandon them at a time of urgent emotional need. This rejection fosters loneliness, desperation, and anger. When divorcing adults with families are thus isolated, they may place their children in the emotional cross fire. I believe that to protect our future—especially our children, our real hope for the future—we need to nurture and support divorcing adults.

THE TRUE NATURE OF DIVORCE

Discrimination is the result of fear and ignorance. But divorce has become a fact of modern life, affecting one out of two American marriages. We do not need to fear such a common, everyday element in our lives. Instead, we need to educate ourselves about its true nature.

Divorce is an emotional journey that follows a course of its own. The stages of this journey—falling apart, separating, trying to cope, coming to terms, and moving on—are all aspects of dealing with loss. With loss comes grief, and grieving takes time. There are no immediate solutions, no quick fixes. The timing is individual. A relationship, a marriage, has to unravel tangle by tangle. The number and size of the tangles are specific to each couple.

The legal aspects of divorce merely punctuate the

process. Just as marriage—the ceremony—is a practical, religious, or legal "period" punctuating the phrase "falling in love," divorce—the legality—is the "period" that punctuates "a change of heart." Traditionally, falling in love is about hope and expectation, and marriage is considered a beginning. A change of heart—the decision to leave your marriage—is about confusion, sadness, anger, loss, and fear, and divorce is considered an end.

DIVORCE IS A BEGINNING

But although divorce may represent an end, it is also a beginning—an opportunity to rise like the phoenix from the ashes. Rather than feeling victimized by the process that divorce puts us through, we can rest assured that the knowledge we acquire from this experience will guide us to future happiness.

In the introduction to *Soul Mates,* Thomas Moore suggests, "When we look at the soul of relationship, we may find positive value in failures, endings, complexities, doubts, distancing, the desire for separation and freedom, and other troubling aspects. We can see these as initiatory opportunities rather than simply as threats."

THE OPPORTUNITIES OF DIVORCE

By focusing on the "opportunities," we can begin to understand the process of divorce and the knowledge it brings us. I believe that the more we understand our feelings, the better we can manage emotional turmoil. If divorce can be an emotional roller-coaster ride, then we need to know how to stay safely seated during a ride that will, no matter how we feel in the midst of it, eventually come to an end.

Divorce is an opportunity to experience the growth inherent in change. From our bodies' ongoing cellular changes to the changing seasons of the year, change in life is natural. The fact that one out of two American marriages ends in divorce may reflect another natural cycle of change. Long-term monogamy is a fairly recent phenomenon. In the past, many marriages ended early due to a high death rate among young adults. Perhaps we should heed Margaret Mead, who wrote twenty-five years ago that if we accepted divorce "as a necessary component of relationships between sexes in a society as complex, as heterogeneous, as rapidly changing, and with as long lived a population as ours, we could then consider how to have good and appropriate divorces."

Divorce is an opportunity to get to know ourselves better, to find out who we are and what we need. It is an opportunity to learn how to forgive ourselves and our spouse for any mistakes we may have made during our marriage, and it is an opportunity to learn from those mistakes in order to refine and define our future. Divorce, then, is an opportunity for personal growth.

MY STORY

Since 1950 and until recently, divorce has been on the rise, reaching an all-time high in the mid-eighties. My parents were part of those statistics. They divorced in 1969 after twenty-seven years of marriage. I was twenty-four. My father remarried immediately after the divorce. In what felt like moments, he began a new life with a new woman, a new rhythm, a new dialogue, a new routine totally unfamiliar to my two brothers and me. My mother, seemingly rejected as she turned fifty, slipped slowly into the unresolved sadness she had brought with her from childhood. A great many of my personal belongings disappeared. My brothers, who were in Vietnam, and I were powerless to salvage any concrete remnants of our family. I felt like a bystander in the trashing of my childhood. Nothing I was morally or physically familiar with seemed to count anymore. From that point on, I felt like a visitor in my parents' re-created existences. At the time I described the feeling as being "on the street corner of life." I no longer knew where I belonged.

To get off the street corner, I married. I was deeply in love with my husband—but I was also angry and in need. I wanted him to transform my life. I wanted him to rescue me. It would have been healthier to start my marriage after I had transformed my own life and rescued myself. But childhood conditioning had taught me that marriage would bring happiness.

My husband certainly transformed my life; he catapulted me into the teeming and often vicious world of politics. Shortly after our marriage, he ran for the U.S. House of Representatives. He lost the election in the last weeks of the campaign due to an onslaught of slanderous publicity generated by his political enemies. It was a terrible blow. We felt bruised and battered by the accusations, and neither one of us knew what to do with the feelings of loss and failure.

On the heels of this experience, I became pregnant. The day our first child was born, my husband started law school thirty-five miles away. Stuck studying in the library until the early morning hours, he often did not come home. I was alone and overwhelmed, abandoned with a new baby in a town that held political disdain for us.

Politics became my husband's life. During the years of our marriage, he was appointed and elected to several political offices. Eventually he was elected to the U.S. Senate. I tried to be happy for him, but after fourteen years as a political wife, I associated politics only with anger, fear, and loneliness. Politics had robbed me of privacy and the right to an autonomous life. As long as I was a political wife, I had to be on guard, carefully monitoring my behavior and appearance in an effort to avoid "bad press," gossip, or the loss of votes. I felt as if I were not just supporting my husband but selling my soul for the sake of his career. I wanted out.

It took two life crises to inspire me to act. The first was severe suicidal depression, which forced me into therapy. In therapy I was able to identify the self-destructive patterns that I needed to change and the tools that I needed in order to change them. The second was the death of my father. Prior to my father's death, like so many women thinking of leaving their marriages, I had been biding my time until I could figure out a way to survive financially on my own. When my father died, I inherited just enough money to keep a roof over my head and put food on the table.

I waited two more years after my father's death before I asked my husband for a separation. Six years and one reconciliation would pass before we actually divorced. Love does not redefine itself overnight.

MY BEST INVESTMENT

After my husband moved out, I raced ahead with my life. I didn't dare look back; I was afraid of what I might feel. I was determined to be socially and professionally successful as a single woman. In the scramble, I often overlooked my two children and deprived them of the vital nurturing and consistency they needed in the face of their parents' separation and impending divorce.

I was separated for five years before I knew myself well enough to be able to finalize my divorce. By then I had also realized that my children were "my best investment." I needed to take care of that investment. My home life, instead of my social life, became my priority.

Making my home life a priority helped me to be quiet long enough to hear my inner voice, a voice that had been clamoring for attention each time I slipped into depression. I realized that if I could live according to the urges of this inner voice, my life would be balanced and rich. So I stopped listening to external pressures to perform and compete. I came home to myself and my children and started focusing on caring for our wounds with compassion and patience.

THE TRAUMA OF DIVORCE

From time to time I meet someone who believes that a divorce is "too easy to get." I ask them, "Are you divorced?" Inevitably the answer is "no!" I have never met anyone *who is divorced* who believes that divorce is too easy to get. Divorce is at the top of the list of life's stresses. Divorce, like death, involves overwhelming loss—the loss of relationship, dreams, the familiar, a sense of security. Divorce, however, includes a perverse twist. Most of us, if we have children, have to revisit the subject of that overwhelming loss—our former spouse—and the dynamics of that lost relationship on an ongoing basis. Each new exposure offers a dose of the old painful realities from which we are trying to recover.

Ending a marriage is traumatic. One common component of trauma is shock. Shock is disorienting and can be life threatening. When we are in shock, we lose sight of who and where we are. Fear and loneliness are also common components of trauma. When divorcing couples find themselves stigmatized and judged by society, these feelings of isolation and guilt are compounded.

WHY I WROTE THIS BOOK

If we encounter someone in shock, we are instructed to wrap them in a blanket to keep them warm and provide them with solace until medical help arrives. I wrote *A Change of Heart: Words of Experience and Hope for the Journey Through Divorce* because I wanted to provide couples and families going through divorce with a blanket and solace while help—counseling, supportive friends, new routines, or the passage of time—is on its way.

Just as in my first book, *You Are Not Alone: Words of Experience and Hope for the Journey Through Depression,* my intent is to offer you the hope, understanding, acceptance, empathy, and support you may not currently have. My hope is that these stories of other individuals who are experiencing or have experienced divorce will validate your own feelings and will help guide you through this process.

The testimonies in this book—composites of the many stories I heard during my travels—validate the wide range of feelings we experience on this journey, and they offer information and support for as long as the journey takes.

I have changed the names, ages, and sometimes the gender of the voices in the stories in order to protect each individual's privacy. You may imagine that you recognize someone you know, but that is because so many situations, stories, and behaviors are common to so many people. If you are a man, you may recognize your own behavior told in a woman's voice, and vice versa. Feel free to change the gender. And if you do not recognize yourself or your story in this book, it does not mean that what you are experiencing is unimportant or invalid. There are so many variables in the process of divorce that it is simply impossible to include them all.

HOW TO USE THIS BOOK

The book is divided into seven sections. The first five reflect the emotional stages of divorce. In the first section, "Falling Apart," we hear the voices of individuals struggling either with the decision to separate or with the unexpected shock of being left. "Separating" shows people facing the logistics and emotional realities of being on their own. In "Trying to Cope," separated or divorced couples share their efforts to manage their new circumstances. The fourth section, "Coming to Terms," includes the stories of adjustment as divorcing or divorced couples learn to get the help they need, accept the changes, and build the foundation for a happy future. The fifth section, "Moving On," documents the final stage in the emotional journey through divorce. Here are the words of forgiveness and hope, the steps that enable us to rebuild our lives and learn to trust again.

The sixth and seventh sections concern outside help. "Finding Guidance and Counsel" contains the wisdom of professionals who work with divorcing couples and families. "Seeking Help" lists individual and institutional resources and provides a bibliography of informative and supportive books. It also includes guidelines for recognizing the signs of domestic abuse and for protecting you and your family from it, and it lists the signs of depression in adults and children.

I recommend reading this book bit by bit. This is a powerful book full of intense emotions. Take your time and if any stories bring up feelings that are hard to bear, stop reading, take some deep breaths, and shift your focus by engaging in an activity you enjoy or that is supportive. Often writing down your feelings or reactions helps alleviate emotions that seem overwhelming.

HONORING THE STORY OF MY DIVORCE

At first I was reluctant to write this book, frightened to look again at my losses and my behavior. I didn't want to dredge up emotions that I felt I had left behind. I had moved on to a new life; I didn't want to revisit my old one.

Now I feel privileged to have had the experience of writing *A Change of Heart*. As always, facing fears and revisiting emotions have turned out to be healing processes. By revisiting my past, I have been able to merge it with my present, and this has given me new hope and strength as I turn once more toward the future. What I am today is a result of what I have learned in my past. To deny parts of my life is to deny parts of myself.

The fact that my life includes my daughters makes this point even more important. I realized that if I rejected the story of my divorce, I would be rejecting not only the story of my marriage but also a large part of the story of my children, for my marriage encompassed their genesis and all the energy that went into it. Their father and I will be their parents forever. In that everlasting fact, he and I remain bonded. Honoring our history is a means of honoring them, as well as myself.

The story of my divorce is their story, too. I may have been the one who made the actual decision to get divorced, but we—the children, their father, and I—were all participants in the journey—before divorce, into divorce, and through divorce. Obviously, we didn't always travel gracefully together. But I, for one, learned a lot.

It was hard to divorce, and it is still hard sometimes, for me as well as for my children. My daughters carry the wounds and wisdom that divorce brought them. For that reason I have dedicated this book to them.

I hope that the words and experiences of the many people finding their way in this book will bring you courage, comfort, and hope. The chaos passes if you let it. The dust will settle if you let it. You can move on if you want to.

I

FALLING APART

Struggling with the

Decision to Divorce

We can only arrive at a new level of experience by means of a painful death in the soul, and what is more painful to the soul than the ending of a relationship?

Thomas Moore, *Soul Mates*

OPEN-HEART SURGERY

Making the decision to divorce feels like open-heart surgery without anesthetic. The emotional pain is so intense it becomes physical. I feel like I'm being cut open, as if my heart is being invaded by cruel, cold instruments.

Molly
age 30

SLOW AND EXCRUCIATING

Everything in my married life has become an obstacle. My relationship is in my way, too.

I've shut down. My body feels condensed, very small, unable to move. I can't sort out my feelings, they're too chaotic. I'm very confused. It is just too much. I try to numb the chaos with alcohol.

I know I should get out of my marriage, but I keep second-guessing myself. Maybe I'm wrong. Maybe it will get better. I read somewhere that some people think it's too easy to get divorced. This is the most painful thing I've ever experienced. It's not easy and it's not quick. It's slow and excruciating.

Laura
age 42

I'M ASHAMED

I don't want to be divorced. I wouldn't feel comfortable letting people know. I guess I'm ashamed or afraid I'll be judged.

People think when you're divorced that there's something wrong with you. If you're a man, they think you're an alcoholic or a wife beater. If you're a woman, you're a nag or frigid. Something like that.

Benjamin
age 27

Scandalous

My husband is emotionally withholding and really criti-cal. Sometimes I'm so depressed I can't get out of bed. The other day I said to myself, "This won't do." The idea of a divorce crept into my mind. But I shut the idea down so fast my head spun.

How can I get divorced? I'm living in Boston. I'm part of an old Boston family. Divorced people are looked down on. They are scandalous. Divorce means failure and shame.

Sally
age 45

OBSESSION

I'm obsessed by the thought of divorce. I never stop thinking about it. I think about it all day, all night. I'm haunted. I've been haunted for three years.

Every time I look at my wife, all I want to do is leave her. She doesn't exist as a person anymore. I think of her as an object to divorce. But I have no idea what to do. How to act on my thoughts? How do I tell this woman I want out?

I don't exist as a person anymore, either. I'm a divorce-obsessed shell of my former self. I need help.

Harmon
age 28

War

I'm just keeping quiet, minding my own business, and staying out of the way. I can't stand being at home because as soon as my parents come home from work all they do is scream at each other. Sooner or later Mom throws something at Dad, stomps upstairs, slams the bedroom door behind her, and doesn't come out for the rest of the night. Dad gets a beer, sits in front of the TV, mumbles swear words for a few minutes, then zones out for the night, too. Half the time he spends the night in his chair.

So where does that leave me? It's as if I don't count. Sometimes I think it would be better if they got divorced. But then, who knows, they pay so little attention to me now, if they got divorced, maybe they'd completely forget I existed. I don't know how I feel.

Kayla
age 16

REFLECTIONS

My husband and I grew apart over the course of twelve years. We weren't able or weren't willing to communicate what we needed from each other. This alienation in my marriage exhausted me. I was suffering from severe depression. I stopped being able to care for myself or to ask for what I needed. And the more depressed I became, the less present my husband was. We drifted farther and farther apart.

Julia

I'M SCARED

I'm scared. I know something is going on, but no one will tell me anything. There's a new kind of silence in the house. Mom's really quiet and she keeps shutting herself in the den and having long private conversations on the phone. Sometimes I know she has been crying, but when I ask, she says, "No, I'm fine, honey. It's just my old allergies." She's never had allergies, so I know she's lying.

I've been counting. It's four times this year that Dad's gone on really long business trips. Or at least that's what Mom calls them. I don't think they're business trips. When Dad goes on business trips, he always brings me presents. When he came back these times, he was empty-handed and strange. Mom and Dad almost act like they're embarrassed with each other.

I feel like a monster is going to jump out of the closet or a bomb is going to drop. I'm really distracted at school. I wish someone would explain what is going on, why things have changed. I'd feel a lot better. I know the news will be bad when I do hear it. But knowing, I think, would be better than not knowing.

Missy
age 12

I Don't Deserve to Be Hurt

I know I have to leave Vince. I know I have to leave because he's sick and I need to protect the kids and me. I know the kids and I don't deserve to be hurt.

But I feel so bad for Vince. He always cries after he beats me up. He says he's sorry. He says he needs me, that he would die if I left him. When he acts like that, I think he needs me to take care of him. How can I leave a guy who's so sad and lonely? And . . . he loves me. He tells me all the time that the reason he gets so upset is because he loves me so much.

I'm getting a lot of help and support from the battered women's shelter. I know I can go there and be safe when I do leave. Everyone has told me that when that day comes, Vince will go crazy. He might even want to kill me. So I have to go to the shelter to be safe. I just don't have the courage to leave yet. I'm still afraid of hurting him.

But you know what? I'm finally even more afraid of being hurt. I can't take this pain anymore.

Clarissa
age 29

I'M RUNNING OUT OF HOPE

My wife says she hates me. Why would I want to stay married to a woman who hates me?

I think I love her, but can I love her if she doesn't want to be with me? I don't think love can go one way. That's like writing checks on a bank account without making deposits. Sooner or later the bottom is going to fall out.

I keep hoping it's just a stage in her life that will pass—that one morning she'll wake up and like me again. But I'm beginning to run out of hope.

I've started getting some counseling from a psychotherapist who specializes in marriage and relationships. I'm trying to get my wife to come to counseling with me, but she won't.

I keep trying to tell myself that getting a divorce might be a good thing. Getting divorced might be an opportunity for me to find someone who does want to be married to me. I guess I'm not psychologically ready yet.

Ian
age 27

CRUEL

My husband and I have decided to separate, but we are still living in the same house. We don't want to lose our rights to ownership. Neither one of us wants to move out until we reach a financial agreement. Our lawyers have advised us not to. If one of us moves out, the court might presume that the person who stayed in the house has more rights to it.

But this is a really horrible situation. Whenever I'm around my husband now, he becomes very silent—almost a zombie. He is shutting down completely, shutting me out of his life. It makes me really angry. I want to jump on him and pummel him. Sometimes I shout at him, "Come alive! Speak to me! Acknowledge me!"

We may be coming apart, but we are still in each other's lives. I think he's being really cruel.

Carla
age 29

I Need to Be a Different Person

I went to my wife and said, "Look, I want to go. I love you to death. I'll always love you, but you know my life has changed. I'm a different person than the man you married seventeen years ago. I need to be a different person."

I'm fifty-five. I'm recovering from a heart attack. My sense of things is different than before I got sick. I feel I am downstream in my life. If I want to do certain things, I'd better start doing them now.

Andrew
age 55

I Can't Move

You know, I'm terrified of leaving. I can't imagine surviving—physically surviving—on my own.

I've even taken my wedding ring off. My husband was devastated when I did. He realized I was serious about not wanting to be married to him. Since then we've developed a new habit. He always wants to talk about our marriage, how to make it work, what he can do, how do I feel. And I can't get out of the room fast enough. So he follows me around the house. Finally, I say I can't breathe. Then he leaves me alone for a couple of days.

The whole situation is suffocating. I can't get out. I just can't bring myself to move.

Leonora
age 34

REFLECTIONS

Soon after I began therapy for depression, I realized that my marriage was unhealthy. I knew in my heart that I needed to separate from my husband, but I thought about it for a very long time before I acted.

I was afraid of many things. Most of all I was afraid of being alone. Even though I had lived alone for five years before I was married, I no longer believed I could manage on my own. I no longer believed that I would be a viable member of society without a husband.

Julia

I Feel Like Trash

He says he's leaving me. Just like that. There's another woman. The blonde—his coanchor on the evening news. I mean, I have to see her every night—this woman who's taking my husband away. I have to see her every night sitting next to my husband making charming little patter.

And he really is leaving. After twenty-five years. Just leaving me. I've kept his house. I've mothered his children. I've entertained all his high-powered guests. I massaged his ego. Don't kid yourself, anchormen have egos! I've done all this for him, and he just up and leaves me for another woman.

I feel like trash. I feel used. Who am I? I mean, who can I be and what is all my caring and dedication if he can just throw it away?

Rachael
age 50

FAILURE

I want to leave my marriage. But it's the second marriage I'm leaving and my parents really like the guy. I called my mother to try and tell her that I was unhappy, that I wanted to leave. She shrieked at me over the phone, "What the hell's the matter with you? Twenty-six and twice divorced!" Oh! Shame. Major shame!

I feel like such a failure now.

Yvette
age 26

Miserable

My wife has made it very clear: if I ever leave her, she'll take the kids and sue me for everything I've got.

Once a month, whenever I can't take her nagging anymore and tell her to shut up, she howls at me, "I'm warning you, buster, you mess with this marriage and you're going to regret it."

How can I leave? She'd fill the kids' heads full of so much angry trash about me. I can't bear to think about the damage she would do. I don't want anything to happen to my kids. I don't want them hurt, and I don't want to lose them.

But I'm miserable. I want out. I just don't know what to do. For the moment I'm seeing a psychiatrist after work. I haven't told my wife, though.

Jack
age 39

VICTIM

My wife is seriously depressed. Twice a year for several weeks, she can barely get up and get dressed in the morning. She's getting psychiatric help and taking antidepressants, but she never gets any better. We've been to couples' counseling for years.

Her medical costs are huge. We have four children who need to be fed and dressed and educated. I'm working two jobs to keep the money coming. On weekends, I work double time driving the kids to movies or Little League games. I'm exhausted and miserable. I feel like a victim. But how can I leave? I feel obligated. I don't think I can abandon this sick woman and my children.

Three months ago, I went for a drink with an old friend from high school. I told him about my wife. He looked at me and said, "You married your mother, didn't you?" I stared at him. He explained, "Yeah, your wife is just as depressed as your mother was."

I left home my freshman year of college to escape watching my father caretake my mother. Now I am doing the same thing.

I love my kids. But I think the best thing for their mental health and future may be to leave this relationship. I'm setting the same example my dad did: victim. I used to love my wife. I've certainly tried hard to help her. I guess the time has come for me to help myself and my family.

Royce
age 52

A Time Bomb

We can't bear to tell the kids that we are going to get divorced. We made the decision a month ago. Now we're living in a time bomb, waiting for the moment we blow the kids' lives apart with the news they are no longer going to have a whole family.

We have three kids: a four-year-old boy, Willy, and a ten-year-old girl, Anna; then there's our oldest, a son, Kipper. He's the one we're most worried about. He's fifteen. He's always been intense and wary. He's never liked transitions or situations that make him feel insecure. Our divorce is going to devastate him.

I dread telling the kids. The prospect makes me sick. It terrifies my wife, Molly, too.

Duncan
age 45

REFLECTIONS

Another reason I waited a long time before I acted on my need to separate from my husband was because I was worried about my children. How do you tell your children that they are losing their security, their sense of family as they've known it? I dreaded seeing the confusion and fear in their faces.

Julia

Too Much Support

My family knows my marriage is in trouble and that my husband and I have talked about the possibility of divorce. They are very supportive and always ready to defend me.

Often this feels good to me and completely understandable. But other times it's too much and doesn't help. They think bad-mouthing my husband is being supportive of me, but it isn't. I married him, and when they put him down, they put me down, too, because they're indirectly saying I made a bad decision.

Krystal
age 37

SIDING WITH THE ENEMY

When my husband and I divorced, my family didn't want to take sides, so they used to have him over with his girl-friends for dinner. That really hurt my feelings. It felt like siding with the enemy. It felt disloyal. I swore I'd never do that to my children.

Now my daughter is thinking about separating. She tells me not to get in the middle, that she is confused enough and my opinions only make it more difficult. But I want her to know I support her. She tells me it doesn't help when I also complain about her husband. Well, she's my daughter and I love her. Therefore, if he's not nice to her, I'm certainly not going to stay quiet. And I'm certainly not going to do what my family did.

Martha
age 68

Trust

We're both strong people, intelligent people. We don't want to believe we lack the power to change things. We cannot imagine, given time and hard work in marriage counseling, that we can't work it out, make it right—because we both used to love each other.

We sit down, either at home or in counseling, and discuss our needs point-blank. We say things like "I need this and this to make me feel like a human being, whole and happy." Or "I know these things are wrong with me, but this is how I am, and you need to like and forgive me."

But we can't do it—we can't forgive, and we can't meet each other's needs.

We've lost the ability to trust one another, and now we've lost the ability to be intimate.

Trust is like the foundation of a building. Without trust, the whole structure collapses.

Arnold
age 39

THE AWFULNESS

Sometimes I think I want my parents to divorce so that I don't have to live with their fighting. Then I get scared. I don't want them to divorce. What would I do? Who would I live with? Maybe I'd have to live with one parent and I'd never see the other parent again . . .

I'm trying to be as good as I can. Maybe that will help them be happy with each other.

Emma
age 10

ANTIRELATIONSHIP

I would rather make it harder for me than to know I made someone else's life miserable.

My wife has just turned on me. She says she wants out. She says I'm a control freak and that I've been dominating our relationship for years. So I've created an antirelationship.

I've become passive. I'm letting her drive the whole thing. She is totally in control. I'm being distant and not very nice. I figure if she really dislikes me, it will be easier for her to leave.

Nathan
age 47

Too Easy

I don't know what is right or wrong anymore. I know I'm just miserable in my marriage. But when I try to talk to my friends about divorce, they all lecture me, saying I'm taking the easy road out, that I should stick with it and work on my relationship. They can't seem to hear when I tell them my husband doesn't want to work on it, too. My husband thinks everything is fine.

Well, everything isn't fine. I don't want to be near him. I haven't wanted to be near him for four years—four hellish years, during which all I've thought about is divorcing him, getting as far away from him as possible.

I just don't know what to do. I want to do what's true to my heart, what feels freeing and joyful. That means leaving my marriage. But I'm afraid of the social reaction. I'm afraid my friends will disapprove and not talk to me. And a lot of them probably won't—all the ones who are in miserable marriages themselves.

It is going to take a lot of courage to leave. I dread the idea of leaving and not getting any support. I don't think I could make it.

This is just awful!

Steffanie
age 28

REFLECTIONS

When I finally decided to separate from my husband, it happened on the spur of the moment. He made some observation that angered me. I snapped at him. He asked me why I had snapped at him. As an answer, I whispered, "I want a divorce." He stared at me and I whispered again, only louder, "I want a divorce."

I don't remember thinking I was going to say that. The words spoke themselves, as if some unconscious voice could no longer be silenced. I repeated the same words over and over again that night. Each time, they took on more character and more determination until finally they were strong enough to become a reality.

Julia

II

SEPARATING

Facing the Reality of Change

No matter how you cut it, divorce is painful. Whether you're old or young, woman or man, rich or poor, the one who leaves or the one who's been left, uncoupling is disorganizing, unsettling, and extremely stressful.

Constance Ahrons, Ph.D., *The Good Divorce*

EMOTIONAL SHUTDOWN

I'm twenty-three and getting a divorce! That's really young. Really naive, really stupid, really depressing.

My wife just left me for another guy. Point-blank. Whoa. Emotional shutdown. A huge betrayal. It's really painful. I don't know how to deal with it yet.

Sam
age 23

I Knew I Was Dying

I sublimated my needs. I did what I thought a good wife should do: I kept quiet and tried harder. I really thought everything would be fine if I just tried harder.

One day I knew I was dying—not physically dying, but mentally and emotionally dying. Well, actually, I think I was scared I was physically dying, too. I felt I might just shrivel up and become so insignificant I'd just wash down the drain with the dishwater without anyone noticing—not even me.

I can't remember when I realized this, but it was very clear. I had to get out of my marriage to live!

Diane
age 52

SLEEPING

Sometime during my marriage I started sleeping. I slept every opportunity I could. I came home from work, had a couple of beers, sat in front of the TV until I fell asleep. After a while, I stopped talking to everyone in my family.

Even on weekends. I remember I used to take my son—I guess he was age ten—to the golf club. I'd have some drinks with the guys at the bar and then I'd sack out on the couch in the men's lounge. I have no idea what my son did during those times.

I slept every opportunity I could because I didn't want to cope with how unhappy I was. I suppose the only difference between me and some guy who stays at the office until late at night to escape his marriage is that I came home to escape.

I didn't wake up until my wife asked for a divorce. But the truth is, I'd left her years before.

Gardner
age 54

I NEED TO PROTECT MYSELF

I haven't told anyone at the office about our separation. I think I shouldn't bring my personal life to the workplace. I don't want people staring at me. I don't want to feel vulnerable or have my boss suspecting I can't do my job.

Jim moved out last week. I went to the office as usual the next day. I'm sure some of my associates suspected something. At a certain point I was standing by the cooler staring into space. I remember being numb. I could think—sort of; I could answer questions and do my work. But it was as if all my movements and actions were disconnected. I didn't know who was going through the paces of my life, because I felt dead all over.

Anyway, I was standing by the cooler and one of the receptionists asked me if I was all right. I answered that everything was fine. I don't think she believed me, but she never questioned. Maybe I'll tell one of my coworkers in a couple of weeks. This is a very competitive atmosphere. I need to protect myself.

I'm just throwing myself into my work—as much to prove to myself that I can survive as to protect my privacy. I hate to admit it, but I have to work harder to do a good job right now than I had to before my separation.

Jessica
age 32

SELF-ESTEEM WRECK

The fact is that bailing out of your marriage is a very scary thing to do. You're confused. You feel like a failure. You're lonely. Your self-esteem crashes—it careens like a skidding car over a cliff.

So, when I was bailing out of my marriage, I went out and hit whatever self-esteem road I thought would keep me on the high road, make me feel better. I'd go anywhere, do anything, to escape the pain. Well, I should have had my headlights on. Because, you know, it was a life that led to another emotional car wreck!

Larry
age 28

REFLECTIONS

When I told my husband I wanted a divorce, when my unconscious voice could no longer be silenced and my unspoken words materialized into sound, it was as if they brought with them a store of resolve and energy.

Suddenly, I had no doubts. Suddenly I knew that if I stayed in my marriage, I would continue to wither as a person. I had to thrive. And to thrive I had to get out of my suffocating marriage. I became focused, desperate, and often irrational about my intent. I didn't think about the consequences. I didn't look left or right. I just forged ahead.

Julia

BAD TREATMENT

I came home from work one day and found a note from my wife saying she'd left and here was her new address and phone number. I started calling her on the phone every day.

Finally she agreed to come back. When she did, I treated her really badly, like I wanted to punish her for making me suffer. So she left again.

Then she came back again. She came back because she wanted to, and I was very grateful. But now it was her turn to treat me badly. That made me be mean again. So she moved out a third time.

She moved in and out several times over the course of a year. Always, we treated each other badly. I'd hit her and she'd throw things at me. Everyone else could see what we were doing, but we couldn't.

I think this separation is final. It's not easy to let go.

Thomas
age 29

LIBERATING

I finally got up the courage to leave. It was just like one of those cartoon drawings—you know, the ones where someone gets an idea and there's a drawing of a light bulb over their head.

Well, one day the light went on in my head! I realized I was being very mean to my husband. He was chasing me around the house trying to get me to talk to him about our marriage, and I was running away from him as fast as possible. That was cruel and disrespectful of him. If I felt suffocated by my marriage and if I was so busy letting him know I didn't want anything to do with him, then what was I doing staying in the house?

So I packed my bags and left in a matter of hours. When I got in the car, I put a Sinéad O'Connor tape in the tape deck and played it as loud as I could. Every once in a while as I drove to town, I took both my hands off the steering wheel. It was wonderful. Wonderful. It was liberating, purely liberating!

Leonora
age 34

EMPTY SPACES

He left last week after twenty-five years of marriage. He told me only a month ago that he was moving in with his coanchorwoman. A month is not a very long time after twenty-five years.

Now I'm rattling around this big house. There are all these empty places where he used to display his personal mementos—awards, bowls, clocks, plaques—he'd received for public service he'd performed, where he had his favorite chair, where his clothes used to hang, where his toiletries were in the bathroom and dressing room.

He's taken all the contents of his office. It's completely empty except for the big TV. He didn't take that because he says "she" has one, too!

I go into his office at 6:00 P.M. when the news comes on. I take a pitcher of martinis and I sit on the bare floor. I watch the two of them on the news and cry. Sometimes I scream at them, but usually I just sit there and sob. I used to feel like trash. Now I feel like trash that's been compacted!

Rachael
age 50

SHUT OUT

My brother and sister-in-law are getting a divorce. For whatever reason, they don't want to talk to me about what is happening.

But I can see what's happening. I can see they are all overwhelmed. I can see that the kids are confused and frightened. I would like to help with the kids. I would like to offer all of them some support, love, and care.

I feel shut out. It's too hard to know what to do or how to act.

David
age 32

They Didn't Like Me

My folks didn't like me, so they're getting a divorce.

Devan
age 5

REFLECTIONS

Telling our children that we were going to separate is one of the toughest things I have ever done. Their father and I did it together. I can remember the terrible sadness I felt.

Our youngest daughter was only six. She says she doesn't remember being told about our separation. But our oldest daughter, who was just nine, has very vivid memories.

It is a moment in our lives that will always feel raw. It still hurts.

Julia

A SPECIAL TIME

We made a special time to tell the kids we were getting divorced. We thought that if we told them at dinner or some other routine family time, it might ruin that time for them forever. We didn't make a big event of it. My wife, Molly, and I just made sure there was a time on the weekend when we were all hanging out together.

My heart was racing, and I know my wife was terrified. We repeated over and over that it had nothing to do with them, that we would love them forever, and that they weren't going to lose a home but gain another.

The kids just stared at us during our little speech. Then Kipper, our oldest who's fifteen, stormed out of the kitchen up to his room, slamming every door on his way. Our eight-year-old girl sat there and cried. Our four-year-old went to the toy box and started playing a game by himself. It was awful.

Finally, we decided Molly should take the younger ones out for pizza. I went up to try and talk to Kipper, but he wouldn't let me in when I knocked on his door. I tried to talk to him through the door, but he kept repeating "Get lost" in this monotone muffled voice.

Kipper still isn't saying much. We're both trying to spend a lot of time with him, but he's really angry. It hurts to see how we've devastated our children's lives.

Duncan
age 45

EXPECTATIONS

My kids are angry that I've left their father. I'm sorry they're angry, but they need to put my decision in perspective.

I was too young when I married. I was nineteen. I had a romantic expectation of my husband. He was this strident, handsome young man with a college degree and lots of ambition.

At nineteen, marriage to that kind of a guy was all I thought I needed. All the magazines I read and television shows I watched led me to believe that if I married the right guy, if I wore the right dress and danced at the right reception, I'd be happily married forever. I remember endless discussions about dresses and flowers for my wedding. But no one talked to me about living together—the domestic details, the financial stress, the emotional ups and downs. No one warned me that happiness wasn't every day.

I'm thirty-five now. I'm a different person than the young girl who married full of dreams. I now know that happiness is a reward for facing the hardships and mundanity. I have different values. I want a life that reflects who I am, not who my husband is. I don't want to settle for an existence.

I don't want my kids doing what I did, either. I want them to have the strength to make their own lives because they know and care about what matters. I'm willing to risk their short-term happiness for long-term strength.

Miriam
age 35

LASHING OUT

My wife was packing her bags the day before she left. She made some comment to me about not watching her terminate a stage in her life. I lost it. I threw her against the wall and screamed at her.

She just fell down, staring at me, big tears rolling down her face.

Sometimes I can't believe what I did. I can still hear her thud as she hit the wall. Other times, I feel so out of control I want to find her and throw her against the wall again.

Divorce is like death. It is full of pain and sorrow. I feel so betrayed, so pressured by so many emotions. I feel out of control. I'm angry. Anger is the only way I know how to express myself. When I'm angry I want to lash out. When I lash out, I feel awful because it's wrong.

I'm a college professor. I'm supposed to know better, and that makes me feel guilty. So I compound my anger.

I'm going to begin psychotherapy before I really hurt someone.

Matthew
age 46

Should I Leave the House?

Should I, the father, leave this child? When we got separated, nobody—not anybody, not even me—asked the question. It was automatic. The guy leaves. Women get the house. The whole legal and social system supports the child staying with the mother. So I left.

Paul
age 36

HALF-EMPTY HOUSES

I hope I can forget this day as fast as possible. The kids' father moved out today. The kids decided that they wanted to help their father move. They wanted to be part of making his new home, of deciding what went where, how their rooms should be. I agreed because I think it is better to include kids. That way there are as few surprises as possible for them.

Thank goodness my husband and I are able to make the kids a priority, that we can keep our disagreements more or less private. So we were able to decide which pieces of furniture to move ahead of time when the kids weren't around.

What none of us realized was the effect that two half-empty houses would have. We were able to be upbeat as a family until we registered the empty spaces. The empty spaces became symbols of the cataclysm our family had just gone through.

Rosemary
age 41

REFLECTIONS

The day my husband moved out, I took the children to visit friends in Maine. We drove two hours up in the morning and two hours back that same night. I didn't want them to see their father moving his belongings out of the house.

I can't remember if I told them what was happening. I was a wreck—short-tempered, overly energetic. I wish we had stayed home and helped their father move. They might have felt more included in the process and as if they had some control in the new form their home life was taking. But I was too overwhelmed to understand that at the time.

Julia

It Isn't Okay

Mom and Dad worked really hard at making their separation okay for us kids. But it isn't okay. Dad looks lonely in his new apartment. And I don't like taking out the garbage at Mom's house. Dad used to do that.

Face it, I'm different now. So's all my family.

Hillary
age 14

AT RISK

I left last week. Vince came home and started screaming at me. I had the two-year-old in my arms. I told him to shut up, it was scaring the baby. He grabbed the kid from my arms and threw him full force into the armchair. I thought he'd broken his neck.

Something in me snapped. I ran for the phone. I hit "0." Vince went for me. I dropped the phone but the operator came on and must have heard what was going on. The police came. I took the kids, the documents, and cash I had hidden and went with the police to the police station. We went from the police station to the shelter. We're going to stay in this shelter as long as we can.

I'm terrified, jumpy. I know I'm at risk. I expect to see Vince exploding through a door any second. I'm sure he's going to try and kidnap the kids. The shelter is helping me with all the legalities I have to go through to protect myself and get temporary custody of the kids.

I'm exhausted and worn out. But I'm not going back.

Clarissa
age 29

Note: If you think you are at risk, please turn to page 177 to determine whether you are in danger and to page 192 for a list of places where you can go for help.

ON MY KNEES

Here I am on my knees—how's that for a metaphor?—packing boxes. Everything I pack has a memory attached to it. I resent every minute of this.

The kids are having a hard time, too. Especially the kid who is away at camp. He knows I'm moving out, but he's not here to witness the process. Poor kid, he's going crazy trying to understand and put some form to his future from a distance.

Karen
age 48

No Money, No Job, No Credit

I couldn't stand my marriage another day. Every single day the guy was drunk. It was abusive. So I split.

The day after, he cleaned out our savings account. I've got no money. I've got no job. No credit. I don't even have the house to fall back on because I left. I've got a lawyer, but I know it's going to be a fight getting a penny out of my husband.

How am I going to support myself? How am I going to eat, let alone pay the bills?

Monica
age 28

Last Act of Married Love

How could I believe that my wife was in love with another man?

I didn't want to believe it. I didn't want to be without her. I loved her. She had been my wife, the mother of our children for fourteen years.

Then one day I realized that, if I loved her, I should want her to be happy. I realized that the last act of married love should be to let her go.

Robert
age 40

REFLECTIONS

I had an excuse for the emotional upheaval, fear, rage, and loneliness I felt. I passed it off on depression, a condition I had been suffering from for several years. It never occurred to me that these feelings were also caused by the loss and grief natural to divorce or that the emotions involved with divorce were compounding my depression. No one advised me, not even my therapist, that divorce was not just an external condition to be disposed of legally but also an internal condition to be cared for with patience, compassion, and understanding.

Julia

III

TRYING TO COPE

Surviving the Transitions

Divorce is unique in that it unleashes our most primitive and most profound human passions—love, hate, and jealousy.

Judith S. Wallerstein and Sandra Blakeslee,
Second Chances

I'm Two People

Sometimes, since I got separated, I feel like I'm two people. It's like standing on one foot or the other. On one I am profoundly delighted, as if the world has opened up. On the other I am profoundly sad and lonely, struggling to survive. It's really weird.

Melba
age 41

I Need to Father

My son, Tim, has moved to his mother's house. I am not able to father him the way I have in the past.

Everyone says Tim needs a father. Nobody says Earl needs to father Tim. But I do. And I can't. At least not right now.

Tim comes to visit me once a week. Stays overnight. He say's it's like going to a friend's house. I figure that's the best I can do right now: be a friend to Tim. Maybe I'll get to be his father again in the future.

Earl
age 45

I Haven't Heard from My Mom

It's been six months since Mom left and I haven't heard from her. Dad says she probably hasn't found a job and a house yet and to be patient.

I'm trying to be patient, but when I go to bed at night I always wonder whether maybe I did something to her and she doesn't like me anymore. Maybe she's sick or hurt. Maybe she needs me. The worst thought I have is maybe she's dead. I wish she'd send me a postcard or something so I know she's all right and still likes me.

I still love her and I miss her.

Peg
age 10

Dreams

Now that we're separated, I'm having incredible dreams. Violent dreams. I'm dreaming about death a lot. But my most common dream is about stumbling and falling. I'm lying on the ground conscious but unable to get up.

Laurel

age 29

SHARK GIRL

My friends called me "Shark Girl"—sharks have to keep moving or they die. So that is what I did for several months after I became separated: I moved. I turned into a kinetic sculpture. I made six to ten appointments a day— early breakfasts, late breakfasts, two lunches, dinners, and any number of business appointments in between. I was manic.

But I couldn't sustain that kind of pace for very long. When I collapsed, I cried for two or three hours at a time. I cried for weeks until I had cried all the feelings of loss and failure out of me. It felt good.

Tina
age 35

We Could Tell Something Was Wrong

I'm very glad Jessica finally told some of us about her impending divorce. We could all tell there was something wrong.

Now at least we can help her. There are many of us in the office who have been through divorces. We know a lot about getting support and advice. I really think that when you go through a life crisis, you need friends around to help you cope. Even for the littlest thing—we all got together and bought her a potted tree to fill up the empty corner in her apartment where her husband's recliner used to be. That's a token of support you can count on at home every day—one that fills the empty spaces, so to speak.

Theodora
age 42

HE CAN DAMN WELL PAY

My friends tell me that revenge will only make things worse. They want me to admit I'm hurt and angry. But if he can just walk out and leave me after twenty-five years for the coanchorwoman, he can damn well pay for it. I'm looking for the toughest lawyer there is so I can get myself a huge alimony. My ex is not going to save any money until he has taken care of me, I'll tell you that!

How do you think it feels to know he's making hundreds of thousands of dollars every year that he's spending on that piece of trash who sits next to him on the news while I'm rattling around the house—the house we built together—every night looking at all the empty spaces he left in my life? Not only that but I have to see his and her faces on TV every night—twice.

I don't care what my friends say, revenge is my way of coping. Just wait till he gets the bill for all the new furniture I'm going to buy for the room that used to be his office!

Rachael
age 50

REFLECTIONS

*During those first years of my separation, as I established
an identity for myself as a single parent and social being, I
felt and behaved like an inflatable plastic punching clown,
the kind with the sand at the bottom. I was down one
moment, up the next, falling to the left, then to the right. I
didn't recognize my behavior. Sometimes my action caused
me to feel embarrassed. I was unstable. To help myself feel
better I practiced saying to myself, "It's okay, Julia, you're
going through a hard time; keep your focus on what you
want and don't want and take one day at a time."*

Julia

I Want to Start Again

I can still remember the moment the light went on in my head and I realized that the decent thing to do was move out. And I will never forget driving away from my house, a Sinéad O'Connor tape blasting from my tape deck, feeling totally liberated.

Once I left, putting distance between my old unhappy life and a new life seemed the most important thing I could do.

I've sold everything I own. There is too much history in our old town. People have such a tight definition of who I should be. People have taken sides—those who believe me, those who believe my husband. Everyone has their version of what happened. And most of them don't approve of my leaving.

I want anonymity. I want to be free. I want to start again.

So, I moved. I have a new job. I'm finding new friends and a whole new way of living in a strange place. It's taking a lot—financially and emotionally—to reestablish myself. But to be honest, tired as I am sometimes, it's worth it.

Leonora
age 34

At the Whim of Somebody Else

I'm asking for joint custody, but every judge in our county dislikes joint custody.

I'm a guy wanting to parent a girl. Thanks to the media, every dad is suspected of incest or child abuse. All my daughter needs to say is that once, just once, I lost my temper.

I've got great temporary visitation rights now. But my ex-wife can go to court at any moment and say, "I want sole custody." She could make anything up to justify her want, and win.

You know what that means? It means I exist as a father at the whim of somebody else.

Paul
age 36

STAYING WITH FRIENDS

When I'm staying in one of my parents' houses, I always feel as if I'm being disloyal to the parent I'm not living with.

So sometimes I refuse to move, to go stay with the parent I'm not staying with. Moving back and forth makes me feel like a yo-yo. Refusing to visit is my way of getting a life back.

Every chance I have I go stay at my friends' houses. It's easier.

Hunter
age 15

READY TO PROTECT ME

I'm not sure how Vince found me. I moved from the shelter in our town to the home of a friend in another town. I think he must have gotten information from our kids' school.

Now he calls me up and screams at me, or he cries. He's been drinking a lot since I left. Once he turned up drunk, shouting that he was going to kill me if I didn't open the door. Luckily, my friend was home. Had she not been, I had worked out a signal with my neighbors. If either I or the kids were alone when he came by and threatened us, they would call the police.

I'm scared for myself and my kids. I know from the local battered women's shelter that I am high risk right now. I'm at risk because he is abusing alcohol, because I have left him, and because he has threatened to kill.

I am doing everything I can to protect myself. The court issued a restraining order. I have left a copy of it as well as a photograph of my husband with the police and with my neighbors. I've now told the truth to the kids' school, so they are protecting all of us.

If he comes by again, he goes to jail. The battered women's support center is keeping an eye out and providing me with moral support. I've started going to Al-Anon at least once a week. There's a whole network of people there who are ready to protect me and who understand.

All this makes me feel less alone, but it doesn't take the fear away. Sometimes I think we might be safer if I went back to him, even though I know that's wrong. Always being afraid is making me sick.

Clarissa
age 29

Note: If you think you are at risk, please turn to page 177 to determine whether you are in danger and to page 192 for a list of places where you can go for help.

WORRIED

The minute you use the word *divorce* in your own life you grow two heads. Everyone around me—even my best friends—treats me with kid gloves. Suddenly I'm a social outcast, a single person, a bad person, a divorcing person!

The irony is I need support. I'm overloaded with emotional questions. My self-esteem is completely undermined by self-doubts. I don't know who I am anymore. I don't know what I want.

I want everyone to know that even if I'm getting divorced, I'm still the same person. I haven't changed. I'm just in shock. I need support. I'm starting to find new friends—friends who are less judgmental and more understanding.

Marcia
age 40

REFLECTIONS

During the first three years of my separation it was hard not to feel judged, stigmatized, and shamed. My conservative neighbors told me a divorcée was dangerous ("You know, Julia, divorcées are potential husband stealers!"), so I was rarely invited to their houses for dinner as I once had been. They also assumed that because I was emotionally fragile, I must be behaving irresponsibly ("Are you drinking your loneliness away?"). And they were accusative ("How can you break up your family?!"). But my close friends were supportive. I tried to spend some time every day with a close friend. Sometimes we took a walk; sometimes it was simply a phone call. Every little bit of caring contact helped.

Julia

I Only Have a Mom

I try not to go near the teacher's desk when she has the book open with all the kids' names and their parents'. I don't like to see my name. Everybody else has a mom and a dad next to their name. I only have a mom.

Luke
age 10

I Need to Get Help

I have a physical reaction if the subject of divorce comes up. I hyperventilate. I want to crawl out of my skin or scratch the inside of my brain. Instead, I eat. I've put on twenty-five pounds.

I'm thirty-eight, and I've already been divorced twice. I can't believe I'm getting divorced a third time. It's incomprehensible, unbelievable. Even when my husband left, I wasn't going to go through with the divorce; I didn't want to face the failure.

My friends say I need to get help. They say I'm depressed. I guess I am. I'm not sure I wouldn't feel like even a bigger failure if I was in therapy. But I'll probably go get some counseling, because I have to do something to feel better.

Sheila
age 38

Disappointed

My family can't understand why I want to divorce this man. He is famous, powerful, and rich—that's all that matters.

My family is deeply into money and power. Their relationship with him makes them look good. They entertain him; they give dinners for him to introduce him to potential customers for his business. They invest in his deals, support his causes.

You won't believe this, but I asked my family for help and they denied me. They're afraid of alienating my big powerful former husband. It doesn't matter to them that he is emotionally and verbally abusive or that he was having affairs during our marriage. It doesn't matter to them that he isn't giving me any money to support the kids or myself.

It hurts to admit that I feel abandoned by my family. But it hurts more to keep looking for their support and being disappointed. For the moment I think I'm not going to spend time with my family. I don't need the feelings of rejection.

Trudy
age 40

USING OUR CHILD AS A PAWN

Why does he want custody? He doesn't even have a job. Not only am I a full-time mother but I've rearranged my job so that I work at home half the time in order to be close to our child when he comes home after school. I work hard to provide for my standard of living.

I'm paying him child support so that he can maintain a house where our child can visit him—isn't that enough? He says my work keeps me from parenting, that he is the houseparent and that our son would be better off living with him because he's a writer and at home all the time. Why is he being so greedy? I think he only wants our child so that he can then get more money from me. I also think he's using our child as a pawn in our divorce. Going for custody is a way of hurting me.

DeeDee
age 38

I Question My Judgment

It's really hard to think about my husband leaving me for another man. It makes me question myself as a woman. I question my judgment.

Having a husband who moves in with a man makes you really wonder what you did. How bad was I as a lover, as a companion? Am I so awful that I turned him off women for life?

Maybe he always liked men more than women. If that's the case, how did I not know it? Will I fall in love with another man who'll leave me, too? What's with me?

I'm also worried about AIDS. Did he use condoms? If he's been able to keep his homosexuality a secret from me, how do I know he hasn't been dishonest in other ways? Maybe he's had male lovers all along and just hasn't told me.

Melody
age 46

REFLECTIONS

Even though I was now a single parent with huge responsibilities, I set my sights on being as socially visible and important as possible. I was determined to act as if everything was "great" and I was invincible. I joined benefit committees and the boards of directors of nonprofit corporations. I commuted from Boston to New York sometimes as often as once a week.

I also dated a lot. Having a lot of men interested in spending time with me gave me a sense of power that I felt I had lost by failing to keep my relationship with my husband together. It wasn't the best coping skill, but it did help me survive my first years of separation.

Julia

WE NEED A FORUM

Our oldest child, Kipper, didn't say much when we told him about our decision to divorce. Now he can barely talk to his mother and me, and his grades have slid into the dirt. He's stopped hanging out with his old friends, and he's defiantly rude in each of our homes.

Things are going from bad to worse. He has started swearing at us. When we get mad and punish him, he retreats more and gets angrier. I know he's drinking and smoking.

I'm having a hard time accepting what we've done to our children. We've basically taken the tectonic plate of their lives and shifted it. Mom and Dad, the pillars that uphold their safety, the structures they've taken for granted so deeply, have been dislocated so completely and utterly. Basically, our kids have experienced an earthquake.

The upheaval is having an effect on my wife, Molly, and me, too. Despite all our efforts to be amicable during our divorce, we are fighting more and more.

We've decided to try family counseling. We need a forum where we can get all the issues out on the table. We need some support and advice on how to handle the trauma to our family.

Duncan
age 45

TIRED

I used to go out at least once a week when I was married; now I'm lucky if I get out once every six weeks. I can't afford the baby-sitters. I always dream I'm going to have friends over for dinner, but that's expensive, and anyway, I'm too tired to cook. One friend suggested I have a potluck. That seems like a good idea, but so far I've been too tired to organize that, either. Face it, handling all the responsibilities of single parenting—the doctors, discipline, finances, homework, domestic details—is exhausting.

Wynona
age 36

I Want to Be Friends with Both

I am close friends with a couple who just broke up. I want to be friends with both, but I can't figure out how to do it. When I call up Tom, I wonder whether I should also call Sue, and vice versa. Will I hurt her feelings if I don't? When one of them tells me details of what's going on in their divorce, I can't empathize as much as I want to. Instead, all I hear are their different versions of a situation, and I wonder if I should explain what the other one said or felt. But I hold back, afraid to sound like I'm taking sides or of being disloyal to one or the other.

I feel as if my once-close friends are becoming simply acquaintances.

Richard
age 57

TAKING SIDES

I wish our friends weren't taking sides. I miss the friends
who have taken my husband's side.

   I'm still the same person, but somehow, now that we
are not together, I've become a monster. They can't be
seen with me in public. I guess they think that would be
disloyal to my husband. I can understand that. What I
can't understand is whether they ever were my friends. I
was very close to some of them. What's happened to those
relationships? Were they just pretending to like me then?
It's lonely. I suppose I should start finding new friends.

Denise

age 28

FOREVER

About a year after my husband and I were separated, I took a trip—the first trip I'd ever taken by myself. I walked by this cemetery in Cambridge, Massachusetts, where a famous revolutionary and his wife were buried. I just stared at their tombstones and sobbed.

I realized that's what I had intended to happen to my husband and me. I thought we would live and die together and be next to each other forever.

Pauline
age 71

Trying to Make It Better

My dad left when I was three and a half. I've never seen him since. The police have been looking for him—I think because he's supposed to pay for me. But they can't find him.

Mom's trying to make it better. She adopted some friends to love me like my dad would have. We call them my "godmother" and "god-dad." I think it's so neat that I adopted a dog, too. I call him my "god-dog."

Matt
age 7

REFLECTIONS

Three years into my separation, three years of trying to distract myself from my loneliness and fear with as intense a social life as possible, I was exhausted. I was running so fast I had lost touch with my emotional, physical, and spiritual needs. When I looked at my two children, I could see they were suffering not only from losing their father but from losing me, too. We were all three in crisis. Something had to change.

I realized I needed to "come home," to focus on my home life and my children. I decided to change my lifestyle. I resigned from all volunteer activities. I no longer traveled. I put my social life at the bottom of the list of priorities. I stopped dating. Free of distractions, I faced some personal truths. I admitted that I was lonely, scared, and needy, and that I didn't know how to be emotionally honest with a partner, my children, or myself.

Instead of running away from my emotions, I met them head on. I learned to meditate: sitting still, using my breath to quiet my mind and body whenever my feelings felt overwhelming. I also started a journal. I wrote something every day; sometimes one line, sometimes ten pages. Through writing I was able to release some of my emotional burden and to document my hopes.

Julia

IV

COMING TO TERMS

Accepting Change
and Finding Hope

Opening to the grief of disappointment and loss, and letting ourselves go through it, allow old dysfunctional structures to dissolve and new wisdom to enter.

John Welwood, *Journey of the Heart*

TREE FROGS

When I got married, everyone rallied around and gave me all kinds of advice and support. Now that I'm getting divorced, even though it is the toughest experience I've ever had, everyone has shut up and disappeared. I don't think they know what to say to me. Talking about divorce is sort of taboo.

One day I got tired of flopping around, feeling lonely. I did a very funny thing. I went into a pet store to look for a kitten to keep me company. But I bought a pair of tiny little tree frogs instead. They are very low maintenance—I can leave for the weekend—and they talk to me. At sunset they start singing. If I make a phone call they sing even louder. So sometimes I just talk to them or sing back. They certainly have plenty to say and I'm not lonely anymore.

Cece
age 36

DIVORCE IS NOT MURDER

Everything I've seen about divorce on TV or in the movies is violent—individuals and their lawyers drawing swords and hacking at each other. It's as if the media image of divorce is the *Rambo* or *Terminator* version of domestic relations.

Divorce may be death, death of a marriage, but divorce does not have to be violent like murder. As long as divorce is adversarial, it will be murder; it will be a violent ending of a relationship. Divorce is about wounded human emotions and broken dreams. Violence will never fix that.

Daniel
age 48

FINANCIAL BONDAGE

I have worked for years so that my wife could have the lifestyle she wanted—country clubs, expensive vacations, nannies for the kids, fancy neighborhood. It wasn't what I wanted. I made it all possible because I wanted her to be happy.

I'm afraid I'll have to provide all this for her forever.

What about me? What if I want to join the Peace Corps, or teach, or retire early, or take a less stressful job?

It feels like financial bondage. I don't think it's fair. She has got to learn to adjust to the changes divorce has brought to our lives.

Frank
age 50

SCRAPING BY

He claims he can't afford to pay me any alimony if he's paying me child support. But his lifestyle hasn't changed at all. In fact, he has a new car, a new girlfriend. He travels all over and with total freedom.

I'm trying to scrape by with just a third of his income. I have three—the two kids and me—to feed and support. I have all the responsibility.

It doesn't even pay to work because if I do, all my earnings go to child care.

He won't even buy clothes for the kids when they're with him. I don't think it's fair. He has got to take responsibility for the changes divorce has brought to our lives.

Elizabeth
age 38

I BITE MY TONGUE

The one thing I don't need to say to my friend is "I told you so!" She keeps telling me one horror story after another about what her husband is trying to get away with in their divorce proceedings. I always knew he was a jerk, but that's a very hard thing to tell a friend. She's disappointed enough. She doesn't need me making her feel worse.

I bite my tongue and keep reminding her that the best thing she can do for herself is to know what she wants and not let her bullying ex intimidate her. She should make sure her lawyer protects her and does what she says. Don't make the ex mad, no unnecessary fights, just take care of herself.

Nancy
age 34

REFLECTIONS

When I decided to change my life and focus on my home and children, I also began to visualize my future. I built the foundation for this future by making some commitments to myself. I practiced finding fulfillment within myself instead of looking outside myself for happiness. I focused on learning what habits I needed to change in order to become an emotionally healthy person. I learned to recognize when I was doing something for external approval instead of really basing my actions on my own beliefs. I practiced having an intimate, supportive relationship with myself so that I could recognize an intimate, supportive relationship with my children and eventually, perhaps, with a man. I prepared myself to be alone for the rest of my life.

It took three years to stop having late-night bouts of loneliness and fear, during which I doubted my decisions and ached with feelings of failure.

Julia

LETTING GO

Relationships have to wind down. You don't just end a relationship and start anew—even after you've divorced. It takes time to change patterns and to let go.

I was furious at my ex-husband for several years during and after our divorce. I couldn't really break away.

As I had during our marriage, I felt saddled with all the responsibilities for our house. Even though we no longer lived together, I would call him up and harp at him about every little thing that needed to be fixed.

Finally, I came to my senses. I accepted my loneliness. I gathered a lot of friends and support around me. I began to live my life without him. I needed to stop expecting attention from him.

Willa
age 34

A Hands-on Father

I have no doubt the media and the law tend to be biased in favor of men. But when it comes to caretaking, the perception is definitely biased in favor of women.

It has taken me two years to make the school aware that I want to be a "hands-on" father, that they can call me, too—not just the kids' mother—if they need a parent. Every year in the fall, I speak to the kids' homeroom teacher, the counselor, the nurse, and the principal's assistant. I also write a letter to the principal. I make sure I'm on the school's mailing list. Then I stay in close touch with the kids, making sure they keep me posted, too.

It will probably take longer to get on an equal footing with my ex-wife. In order for me to be there for the kids, she will have to let go. She will have to be able to say to herself, "He's okay as a parent even though I didn't want him as a husband." For the moment, I don't think she believes I can care for the kids as well as she does.

Wallace
age 37

The Real Way to Share Custody

I'm glad my parents share custody, because I need to be able to see each one of my parents whenever I want to. But I don't like going from one house to another. As soon as I get settled in one place, I have to move to another. One of the ways I cope is by biking back and forth on my own time. At least I'm in charge of the change.

The real way to share custody is not for one parent to move out but for both parents to move out. Then the parents could take turns being with their kid in the *kid's* house!

Serena
age 15

FAMILY THERAPY

It was a good move to start family therapy. Our oldest boy, Kipper, is beginning to mellow out. He's not so withdrawn. He's able to tell us how angry he is that his mother and I destroyed his trust. And we are able to hear it without feeling too defensive.

We've also solicited the help of the counselor at each of our kids' schools. They have provided us with suggestions and recommendations on how to be positive and how to manage the rough spots. They can also keep an eye on the kids. In our daughter Anna's school there is a group of kids whose parents are divorced or divorcing that meets once a week to talk about the issues they are trying to deal with. Anna doesn't feel so isolated and alone.

For Willy, our four-year-old, the issues are different. He feels the upheaval but doesn't understand what divorce is all about. One of the school counselors gave us a list of children's books for his age group that explain what is happening to his family.

Our goal is to show our kids again and again that even if we are apart, they are safe. We need to reassure them that we are doing everything to make sure they don't fall between the cracks.

Duncan
age 45

REFLECTIONS

My ex-husband worked in another city. He usually came back to Boston on the weekends, but not always. Some separated or divorced parents are able to divide the time they have with their children more or less equally, but I didn't have that opportunity.

Children need constant attention and care for their health, their homework, their social skills, their struggles to learn about life. The more children the more time a parent must commit to guiding and supporting them. When you are alone as a parent, the time demands are unforgiving. The parent has little time to recover from one emotional or physical demand before a new one crops up.

I learned that it was a waste of energy to resent the demands on my time. It was better for all of us—the children and me—if I embraced my responsibilities. I knew that all too soon the children would be leaving for college, relationships, or jobs. I might as well put my whole heart into parenting them full time while I still could. I suspected I would regret anything less once they had "flown the coop."

Julia

SAFETY

I didn't feel safe for a long time after my parents divorced and sold our house. Everything I knew and counted on—our garden, our neighborhood, the routine in our house, knowing what to expect, feeling protected because my parents were both in the same bed down the hall, a sense of belonging—dissolved when the house was sold.

I'm beginning to trust more. I'm in college and I live off campus with two friends. Taking care of my own house has given me some control over my safety.

Jemma
age 21

A COMMUNITY OF FAMILY

Instead of referring to children of divorce as members of "broken" families, we should look at primal societies.

I know a Native American woman who says that there are no such terms as "broken" or "extended" for divorced or remarried families in her culture. She says the word for all her father's brothers is "father." She says a child does not have to be left out when his or her immediate parents divorce. The child can be included—included in a larger family.

I agree with the idea, but the trouble is, we all move around so much and our sense of community is so fractured. My brother lives in Maine. He's not available to my children, so I am trying to enlarge my child's sense of family by creating a community of family with my friends.

Marcus
age 40

Together Again

When Nicholas and I first decided to get divorced, we felt very sure about our decision. We had talked about it a lot. We had gotten some couples counseling. We thought we were being very sophisticated about the whole process.

About a year into our separation, we went to dinner together. We had a great time. It felt so good and safe to be with each other. We went back to my place—our old home—and made love. That felt safe, familiar, and good, too. So we decided we should try living together again.

What a mistake! This time it was harder to come apart. The second disappointment was piled on top of the first.

What we both understand now is that it is hard to start all over again—dating, meeting people, building a community of friends on your own. Sometimes you can kid yourself that being in an old bad relationship is better than being on your own.

Geena
age 31

SECOND THOUGHTS

When my husband left me after twenty-five years of marriage for his young coanchorwoman who does the news with him, I really wanted revenge. But I'm not sure that's how I feel right now.

I'm not sure I've hired the right lawyer. There's no question my lawyer's as tough as I want him to be. I hired him because he told me that my ex should pay me so much alimony he wouldn't have anything left to put into his retirement fund for at least ten years. At the time, that sounded like a fair financial deal.

But . . . I'm having second thoughts. The whole process is useless divorce gamesmanship. It just seems to escalate in aggression and cost. It's so consuming. I feel as if I'm caught in a legal whirlwind. I feel victimized by my lawyer. He keeps spouting legal terms at me about what I should do. Sometimes I doubt it's all necessary. I feel as if I should know more about divorce law so my lawyer doesn't push me around so much.

I'm spending all this time, money, and energy, but I don't feel any better. I'm still angry. I'm still hurt. I still feel rejected. I don't think a legal battle wins the emotional war. And right now, what I'm experiencing the most are overwhelming emotions. I think there must be other things I can do for myself to feel better.

Rachael
age 50

REFLECTIONS

Divorce, I thought, was only a matter of legal and financial details. Not knowing any better, I looked for a "tough" lawyer. In retrospect, buffeted by the divorce process, I was unable to differentiate among my legal, financial, and emotional needs. What I was really looking for was someone "tough" enough to protect and support me. Of course, that is not the role of a lawyer.

I also looked to a lawyer to tell me what I wanted and needed. Again, in retrospect, I realize that I had my head in the sand. I was too emotionally overwhelmed to want to come to terms with what I deserved or was legally entitled to. What I really needed was to take action and inform myself about divorce law. Instead, I sat passively by, dependent on the judgment of a third party. It didn't take long for me to realize that the lawyers had made a deal that worked for themselves, not for me.

I wish I had known about mediation—it might have saved us a lot of time, stress, and money. A good mediator would have insisted I come into the negotiations prepared—knowing the law and what I wanted and needed financially and emotionally—and would have made sure that the negotiations were always equitable. I would have been obliged to engage in the process of my own divorce, a process that would have helped me focus on building a stable future.

Julia

Hiring a Lawyer

I postponed hiring a lawyer. I think I postponed it because there was such finality to the act. You know: this is it, now I'm really going to be divorced.

My husband served me with some legal motion. Then I had to get my act together. Where to start?

I asked several divorced friends if they knew of any lawyers. I got a list of names. The first lawyer I talked with scared the daylights out of me. He was a real barracuda, suggesting ballistic tactics that intimidated me. I felt like he'd eat my husband for breakfast—something I didn't want—and probably me, too. I called another one, but she was so expensive. A third never returned my call.

So I decided to go to the library and ask the librarian to help me research information on divorce. And I used the Yellow Pages of the phone book to find divorce support groups, legal services, and lawyers who specialized in domestic relations.

I found out that there are divorce mediators who help you reach an agreement with your spouse outside the legal process and without aggression. There are also "collaborative" divorce lawyers—lawyers who work together rather than against each other to get an equitable settlement. This was more my speed.

The next step will be to shop around for fees and personality. I figure that if I am going to have to share details about my life with this stranger and spend my hard-earned dollars, I better like the way he or she treats me.

Caroline
age 43

PLACES OF AGREEMENT

Obviously, if my wife and I are divorcing, we aren't getting along. At first we hired lawyers to negotiate our divorce settlement, but every time we met with our lawyers we fought more. We fought about property. We fought about custody of our children.

One day my wife called me and said that she needed to tell me how she felt. She was frustrated. She said, "We didn't spend our marriage in the lawyer's office, so why are we spending our un-marriage in the lawyer's office?"

That hit home. I realized divorce has two levels. The primary level is the personal, emotional one. The secondary level is the legal one. We had married because of an emotional commitment; we needed to un-marry that way, too.

I also realized that the lawyers were defining what our relationship had been without ever having met us before our divorce. I wanted to be accountable for my own decisions, consistent with how I had lived my marriage.

That's how we discovered mediation. Through mediation my wife and I are able to identify our places of agreement—an important process in order to protect and care for our children. We've kept our attorneys to advise us legally, but the main thrust of our negotiations is to agree on our children's needs.

It isn't always easy. We both slip into blaming the other for our failed marriage. In the end, though, we realize that focusing on the other as the bad person is not going to serve either of us—and it especially won't help our children.

Ross
age 47

I STOPPED NAGGING

In the first months after our separation, I was always calling up the children's father and asking him to come and get the kids. He never could be consistent. I could never count on him. I would stand at the kitchen telephone and demand, "Come take these children. Be with these children."

Then I realized that the more I insisted on his coming and the more he failed, the more the children felt rejected. They felt rejected by his absence. They felt rejected because I appeared to want to get rid of them.

Finally, it dawned on me. If he wanted to be a father, he would have to be one of his own accord. I couldn't make it happen. I stopped asking. This also meant the kids no longer heard me yelling at their father on the phone. Kids don't need to have rejection of any kind rubbed in their faces.

I think the children are coming to trust that they have someone to count on. They know they are always welcome and wanted at home with me. When and if their father shows up, they are free to be with him as long as he respects their schedules. Maybe the erratic appearances their father makes will begin to have some consistency, too, because ironically, now that I have stopped nagging, their father is taking more and more responsibility to see the children.

Natalie
age 43

The New Situations Are Better

I'm not sure I agree that divorce is bad for kids. I mean, yeah, it's true that Mom and Dad's divorce has messed my life up. I'm having to make a lot of adjustments I don't want to make—new homes, new men and women in their lives.

But I'll tell you something. The new situations are better than the actual family situation that existed when my parents were together. I used to smoke a lot of dope. I swear it was because I was so miserable at home. I hated my house and them so much that all I wanted to do was zone.

They are each a lot happier in their new homes and lives. I don't know if I care about the people they're dating yet. But Mom and Dad are much more pleasant to be with, and that's okay by me.

So if you ask me, I'd say that two half-families that are getting along are a lot better for a kid than a whole family that doesn't.

Hank
age 21

REFLECTIONS

Children do not flourish if they hear continuous arguing within a marriage. They truly suffer when they hear continuous arguing outside a marriage. Children often think they are the reason the relationship came apart. Arguing outside a marriage, which usually has to do with something directly related to the children like custody or child support, only convinces them of that guilt.

Even though my ex-husband and I tried, we were no different from many divorcing couples. I, for one, deserve no medals for responsible arguing—that is, arguing with my ex only when I was sure my children could not hear.

We were great at something else, however. We always respected rituals and children's events—Christmas, graduations, sports competitions, plays, birthday parties, illnesses, and so on. We came together with pride, unanimity, devotion, and unilateral support. All disagreements miraculously disappeared when it came time to stand by our children. I am very proud of both of us for that.

Julia

HOLIDAYS

I really came to terms with the reality of our divorce at Christmastime. Especially the first Christmas. I woke up all by myself instead of being woken by the raucous overexcited voices of the kids who wanted to tear downstairs and open their presents. I remember that heartrending silence that first Christmas by myself.

Then I realized that it was probably just as hard for the kids not to have me there. So I picked up the phone and called my ex-wife. We agreed that it would be good for the kids' sake if I came over.

So I took some clothes in a little bag, put a raincoat over my bathrobe and pajamas, and drove over to our old house. I walked into the kitchen determined to be as natural as possible—even if I was dying inside.

We all tried very hard to be cheery. We did a good job, but we all knew we were trying.

After that first Christmas, being together for special occasions and holidays got easier. My ex-wife and I looked beyond our awkwardness and focused on making the children feel as important and included as we could. After all, I see no reason to ruin Christmas, or birthdays, or graduations, or recitals for your children because you no longer live with your wife. These are child-oriented events, and therefore, the focus should be on making them as magical and memorable for the kids as possible.

Edward
age 49

NASTY

Kids have a right to care about each parent, whether the parents care about each other or not. The trouble is that couples play out the illness of a marriage in a divorce. And if there are children, then the kids are the field the illness is played out on.

I know. I am always putting my wife down in front of the children. I harbor resentment and anger at her for breaking up our marriage. I want the kids to feel the same way. I want them to think she is a bad person and I am a good person, or at least a wronged person, a person wronged by her. I want them to punish her by loving me more.

This is a nasty thing to ask of my children. Divorce is hard on children, but it shouldn't destroy them or their sense of family. I'm getting counseling from a psychotherapist so that I can start to heal my anger.

Stuart
age 35

REALITY SLAP

When the light went on in my head and I realized the decent thing to do was to move out, I thought I was free. When I moved to a new town, got a new job, and met new friends, I was sure I had put my marriage behind me.

Then came the reality slap: I found out from my mom that my ex got married. The news was like a knife in my heart.

I thought all these months that I was totally in charge of all my feelings. When I got the news, I felt really rejected. It brought back all those feelings of terror, of fearing I couldn't survive on my own, that I'd had before I left the marriage. I felt angry. Who did he think he was, getting married ten months after our divorce?

Finally I realized I needed to do some grieving. Whether I'd liked my marriage or not, my divorce was a loss. My new friends were great. They encouraged me to cry—they even took me to sad movies!

Leonora
age 34

I Wised Up

I don't mind admitting I was the stereotypical divorcée. When I got married, I stayed at home and was a housewife. I forfeited my employment track record by giving up my job for marriage. I linked my identity to being a wife and mother. Then I got left, suddenly, because he didn't want to be married anymore.

My husband, trained as a go-getter, went to the office, hired a hotshot lawyer, and acted as if our divorce were a matter of completing another venture-capital deal. I was at home, feeling victimized, behaving like a Ping-Pong ball, bouncing back and forth between moods. For a while I did everything he told me to do, including hire the lawyer he recommended to represent me in our divorce. After all, I thought, he's the man out there in the big world; he'll know what I should do.

One day a friend handed me a divorce workbook she had used for her divorce. On each page were helpful hints and instructions on how to protect myself. I realized that a guy who left me without much reason and who was treating our divorce as nothing more than a deal was probably also a guy who was interested in his own well-being, not mine—even if we had been married for ten years.

I wised up. I read the book from cover to cover. I made a list of my assets and needs. I found a really smart woman lawyer. I got temporary work to earn enough money to pay my legal fees. Now I no longer feel victimized, and I'm gaining back my self-esteem.

Lydia
age 47

REFLECTIONS

During the early years of my separation and divorce, my family was silent. Some members of my family even seemed to be better friends with and more loyal to my ex than to me. I felt that no one in my family offered me any financial or legal advice or support. Emotional support was served up in drops. This family silence made me feel abandoned and hurt.

I was on my own, scrambling around trying to figure out how to hire a lawyer, pay the legal expenses, and manage a family. I made a lot of mistakes. But I also grew up. I learned from my mistakes and eventually became very proud of my ability to cope.

Julia

I Feel Safer

Vince sort of ran out of steam once the divorce was over—just as the counselors at the battered women's shelter suggested. That may also be because the court ordered him into counseling. Anyway, he doesn't threaten me anymore.

The kids and I have moved back to my parents' town. I feel safer being near my parents. I was afraid my husband might follow me here. I had been warned that men who batter women sometimes stalk them.

The move and the divorce have not been easy on the kids. There's good counseling at the kids' school, which helps, especially with my oldest. She's sixteen and acting out. I think she may be drinking. I know she's smoking. She's gotten in a lot of behavioral trouble at school.

The fact is my kids have been abused, too. A kid who witnesses violence is a victim of abuse, and my kids saw their father hit me many times.

Luckily, there's more than one support center in town. There is even one for families, which is good because as a family, we need to learn new ways of relating to each other that don't involve screaming and hitting.

Sometimes it feels overwhelming. But then I remind myself of how far we've come already. I know there's support out there. I've gotten it. I know I'm not alone. I know I'm not the first woman to leave a husband who beat her. I know I can help myself and my family. So I keep trying.

Clarissa
age 29

You Can Still Be Great Parents

A lot of our friends don't understand. They look anxious and say, "You guys are such good parents. You work so hard and closely together for the good of your kids. Why do you want to get divorced?"

I believe you can be perfectly good parents without loving one another. Parenting is about loving your children, not about loving each other.

One of the reasons my ex and I were able to divide up our household possessions with no rancor and very little disagreement was because we let the kids choose what they wanted in each house. We laid some ground rules. For example, my ex and I kept heirlooms from our respective families. And if the kids disagreed on what piece of furniture should go in what house, we would draw straws. The winning child got to decide what house, the losing child got to decide the fate of the next item that there was some disagreement over. The process wasn't stress free, but it certainly gave us all a sense that we were a coherent working organization, not a polarized rabble. And the kids felt like they had some control over the physical form of their future.

Tersch
age 40

LATCHKEY KID

I'm a latchkey kid, like a lot of kids from divorced families in my school. We all have keys to our houses and go home on our own. Usually I have some chore I have to do when I get home—Mom wants me to put the chicken in the oven or something. Sometimes a bunch of us hang out at the local pizza parlor. It's a way of feeling less left out. Most of us who live in divorced households have less money than other kids, especially if we live with our moms. That means we don't get to go to special activities after school.

I don't mind being a latchkey kid. It's kind of cool because I have more independence than the rest of the kids in my grade, so I'm kind of important. But I do mind having to give up guitar lessons. Mom and Dad both say they can't afford it. I'm saving my own money, but I kind of resent losing the opportunity because they couldn't get their act together.

If I think about it too much I get angry, so I try not to think about it.

Jessie
age 15

Divorce Support Groups

Someone once said it takes a year to get a legal divorce. If that's the case, then it takes eight years to get an emotional divorce.

It's very lonely when you are getting divorced. It would help to be able to go somewhere and share information and experience.

If there were divorce support groups such as AA for alcoholics, the whole process could be sped up and the pain of it eased enormously. I've heard there's an organization called Divorce Anonymous, but we don't have a group in our town. One of these days I'm going to find out how to start one.

Holly
age 46

AS POSITIVE AS POSSIBLE

It's amazing how financially destructive divorce can be. Before our divorce we had a great house with plenty of room for our sons. Now we're both shoved into our respective little condos, everybody piled on top of everybody else.

The cash flow is depleted, too. We used to pool our resources. Now everything is divided. Plus I'm paying my ex-wife child support to help her maintain her household, as well as shelling out to maintain my own.

I keep trying to remind myself that I'm lucky to have a good job, that I survived this kind of financial hardship before when I first started out, that the boys will learn how important budgeting is, and any other benefit I can think up to help buffer these difficulties.

When I'm alone in bed at night, it's very easy to beat up on myself by rehashing all the mistakes I feel I made that contributed to the breakdown of my marriage. When my mind heads in that direction, I try to reverse the thought process and forgive myself.

Each day that passes makes it better; I feel more and more in control of myself and my finances. I know in time that if I keep working at it, everything will be resolved and we'll feel settled. In the meantime, I need to be patient and as positive as possible.

Tony
age 48

REFLECTIONS

The divorce process asks much of a single parent with a young family. There are, to name a few, ongoing legal decisions, financial decisions, domestic details, schedules—social, academic, personal—for both the children and the parents. It was very easy for me to forget what I needed, faced with all these demands on my time and energy.

With the help of my therapist, I learned to begin focusing on my needs, too. There were several things I did to help myself. The first was to identify and act on my dreams and desires. I had always wanted to continue the dance lessons I'd started as a young girl, and I had always wanted to write. So I found a ballet teacher who would take a thirty-six-year-old student, and I signed up for Radcliffe Seminar poetry workshops. These became oases during my single years in Boston.

The second thing was to make a plan for the future: where and how I wanted to live when my children left home. My dream was to move west to a small community surrounded by nature. I wanted to leave behind all the "shoulds" and restrictions of big-city East Coast living. I wanted to be my strong and independent self, free of the shadows and complications of politics. Like generations before me, I felt the West would offer a place to begin.

Finally, I made a list of what I wanted in a man and a relationship, and I vowed not to compromise until the right one appeared, if he appeared.

Julia

V

MOVING ON

*Learning to Forgive, to Rebuild,
and to Trust*

What we call the beginning is often the end
And to make an end is to make a beginning.
The end is where we start from.

T. S. Eliot, "Little Gidding"

In Search of a Destination

The day after my divorce became final, I got in my car and started driving. I drove all over Wyoming, Oregon, Washington, California, Nevada. Maybe I even got to Arizona. I don't remember. I just drove. I had no destination. I didn't stop to visit anybody. I just drove from town to town, from motel to motel, or I spent the night camping off the road. I can't tell you what I saw or where I was going. I was just going, leaving my pain behind at every stop.

Jean
age 31

SOUL WORK

Somebody once told me that suffering was soul work and that soul work was done in the "valley." Well, divorce is soul work, and you spend a lot of emotional time at the bottom of a valley.

You can get out. You can climb out. But you also have to take responsibility for your pain. Granted, it's easier to blame your partner for all the pain you feel. But if you don't own up to your own feelings, you can't grieve. If you don't grieve, you can't move on wisely.

Once you're wiser, you can begin to think about constructing a new life for yourself, a life free of a relationship that must have been emotionally draining if it was unhealthy enough to come apart.

The point is to keep your eye on the goal of moving out of it, moving beyond. Once you've moved on, you're better off. You earn a lot of self-esteem. You know you can survive one hell of a challenge.

Theodore
age 35

Basic Emotions

Divorce may be the most intimate part of a marriage. To get divorced successfully, you have to look with courage and honesty at what went wrong in your relationship. You have to face some very basic emotions together.

When you understand what went wrong, you also understand what you need and want. When you know what you need and want, you know what to look for in a new relationship.

Lon
age 57

SHE CAN'T ACCEPT MY ANGER

My stepmother can't accept my anger. I get angry when I have to pretend life is all about happy little dinners with her and my father.

I have tried to tell her that I come from a divorced family and that no matter how "healthy" my family's divorce was, there is a lot of loss. That loss has to be taken into consideration. I live the loss every day of my life. I don't think I let it get in my way because it is part of who I am and I've gotten used to it. But my stepmother needs to accept my experience.

Jessica
age 18

Finally Free

We couldn't end it, we couldn't actually do the grieving to say good-bye. Even after our divorce, we'd call each other up and continue the same destructive relationship *outside* our marriage that we had had *inside* our marriage!

I think if we had had counseling together during our separation and divorce, we might have understood what we were doing to each other. As it was, it took a long time to really come apart. I just thank my lucky stars we never had children. Our constant haggling would have destroyed them.

It wasn't until his job took him to another city—away from where we both lived—that we were able to move on into other healthy relationships.

Now we are each remarried. More important, we are friends, although we rarely talk or see each other. Our spouses are friends, too.

I finally feel free, and so does he.

Gail
age 39

REFLECTIONS

It was hard to terminate my marriage finally, to stand before a judge and agree that "a divorce from the bond of matrimony be granted ... for the cause of irretrievable breakdown."

A friend went with me. As we drove away from the courthouse after I had met with the judge, I remember feeling as if I'd been launched into outer space and was floating free of gravity. Now I wish I had created some ceremony to honor the passage, marking the ceremonial end as I had marked the ceremonial beginning with a wedding and reception.

Julia

DIVORCE PARTY

My ex-wife and I got together with our kids and close friends and had a dinner party after we'd finalized our divorce. We wanted to commemorate our union, celebrate the good things, our kids, our happy memories. We felt that there had been so much hoopla about our coming together that it was odd to let our coming apart just fizzle.

We laughed together. One of our friends called it a "Coming-Out Unpartnered Party." We toasted our past, our future. There were also some tears. For the kids it was an opportunity to see that they were still very much a part of a community of people who understood and supported what they were going through. For my ex and me, it was a way of honoring our past together and of giving our family and our friends permission to participate in our future.

Perry
age 37

Tree Roots

If you have children, divorce is like cutting down an old tree in your front yard. The tree disappears, but the root system is still there.

After I got divorced, I thought I could start all over again, make everything neat and tidy—you know, the way you can clean up your yard by mowing the lawn carefully. But I had three kids—the roots between their mother and me.

In time, I came to accept that my yard had a root system growing through it, so to speak, that was permanently entwined with my ex-wife. Instead of trying to ignore her or make her disappear, I needed to find a way to acknowledge her role in my history. After all, the man I am today is because of my experience with her. By welcoming her role in my history, I found yet another way to welcome my children in my future.

Hank
age 35

SECOND-GUESSING

For a while I was very confused. I enjoyed being in my ex-husband's company.

For the kids' sake we would get together on holidays or special occasions—graduations, prize days at school, sports events. We would all laugh and have a good time. It was really important for the kids . . . but hard on me.

I would feel this twinge in my heart. I would second-guess myself and wonder if we should have divorced. The emotional confusion was painful, so I'd get defensive, rude, and distant. It felt safer that way.

Slowly I began to accept that those feelings were always going to come up when I saw my former spouse. As I got used to them, I stopped fighting them. Then I realized that they were probably good feelings because they were a way of honoring the years we had spent together and the family we had created.

My former husband and I have become two very different people with very different lifestyles and priorities. We have new lives and new spouses. But by being sentimental about our prior life together, we can integrate our past with our present. That integration lends validity to the experiences we had together—especially the experience of parenting. It's healing for us and healing for our kids.

Kathy
age 37

COMMON BONDS

Mom and Dad may be divorced in a court of law, but they're not divorced in a court of parenthood. You can't have a kid with someone and then get divorced. I'm a common bond between my parents.

When I was younger, I used to dream that Mom and Dad would get back together again. I remember trying to put their hands together as if that would glue them to each other and, of course, me.

I was eight when Mom got remarried. I didn't understand. My stepfather moved into our house and Mom's bed. The first night I saw him unpacking in Mom's room, and I asked, "Where's Mom going to sleep?" Then they explained to me that my stepdad was going to sleep *with* Mom in *her* bed where Dad used to sleep. I was really upset. I had to realize Dad was never coming home to Mom's house.

I know in my head that Mom and Dad are never going to get married again, but a part of me wants to hold on to the past. The way I've been able to deal with the changes in my life is to know that they will always be together as my parents. Being my parents is separate from who they are in their business lives and new marriages.

Chelsea
age 15

PROTECTING THE BALANCE

I'm not interested in marrying again. Not now. I'm very interested in my own process. I'm very interested in raising my own children.

I've just established a balance in my personal life I can support—my relationship with the man I'm with now, my relationship with my ex-husband, my relationship with my children, my relationships at work. I need to protect that balance and work toward creating an even safer environment for myself. That safer environment is only going to come through my own development, my own process, my own efforts to take responsibility for my life.

So, I'm not ready to get married again.

Ruth
age 27

REFLECTIONS

As a single parent I needed to develop a cooperative relationship with my children. A hierarchical setup with me as the sole authority wasn't going to work. My children were too frustrated, angry, and pained by their losses.

I needed to listen, to hear their opinions, to look beyond bad behavior. I focused on using compassion, on trying to look beneath their superficial criticisms to the pain below. I tried not to focus on the symptoms but to look for the causes.

It wasn't always easy. It took several years to learn a cooperative model for living together. In fact, we are still perfecting our ability to listen.

My children also saw that I loved them with the ferocity of a she-bear. No one messed with my kids without contending with me! They knew they could count on my love—no matter how exaggerated and comical my ferocity could sometimes be.

Julia

A COMPLETE TURNAROUND

Kipper has made a complete turnaround. Family therapy has given him the forum to express his fears and concerns. It has also given us a safe place to tell him our needs. He has come to understand loss. He's beginning to trust again.

His mother and I are very proud of him. We don't hesitate to tell him how we feel about the person he is becoming. You can almost see him physically developing strength of character. He is also recycling his newfound wisdom by helping other kids, not only in our family but at school. Once a week he goes to the counseling office at school and talks with peers or younger students who are going through divorces. I think he can see how positive his experience is compared to some of the other kids' situations.

Divorce is not easy on kids. But I believe stress and pain can make kids more empathic to others and more resilient. Only you can't minimize its effect. As parents, you have to own up to the cataclysm you've created in your children's lives. You have to provide the support kids need in order to bear that stress and pain.

One of the ways we've provided that support is by understanding who we are as a family regardless of whether we are married or not. Family therapy has been essential to that process.

Duncan
age 45

Two Sides to Every Story

I feel very badly about how I treated my father during my parents' divorce. When my mother discovered his affair, she was so hurt. It wasn't hard for my brother, sister, and me to feel outrage. We were all in our late teens and early twenties. It was terrifying to think that suddenly, without any notice, our father had done something that was threatening the well-being of our family. He seemed like a traitor.

I was furious. I was the oldest son and I felt responsible for the family. When Mom threw Dad out of the house and he moved in with the "new woman," as we called her, I wouldn't see him or speak to him.

I wrote him one letter in three years. I sent it while they were still negotiating their divorce. I wrote, "This is to let you know that how you treat Mom in the settlement will be indicative of how I treat you in the future."

I didn't see him until the first Christmas after I got married. I took my wife to meet him. I didn't bring him a present. I still didn't think he deserved any. I wince when I remember saying something like, "You know, Dad, we think about having children and we think about having them around you and we don't want them to be around you."

I've been married ten years now. I've experienced first-hand the ups and downs of relationship. I realize that Dad wasn't the only one to blame for the breakdown of his marriage. There are two sides to every story.

I apologized to Dad several years ago, and he apologized to me. It will never be the same as it was before my parents' divorce, but we're working hard at building a new friendship. Family is important, no matter how you define it.

Jake
age 32

LOVE ISN'T ENOUGH

I try to keep reminding myself that there is a difference between loving someone and living with them. Just 'cause you love someone doesn't mean you should live with them. If you have a destructive relationship, as we did, then you shouldn't be living together. Even if I think I still love him.

I have to silence this nagging voice I hear in my head that wants to convince me I could have made him happy if only I had been a better wife. The voice tries to whisper, "It's your fault he got so angry."

Thank goodness I've trained a louder voice that screams, "No, it's not!" Thank goodness I have a support system that reminds me of all the physical and emotional pain the kids and I have been through. Because sometimes, especially when I'm lonely and overwhelmed, I really want to go back.

My support system is also important because it's hard to hear people shame me. People say things like, "How could you have married a wife beater?" I know they mean to be helpful, but it makes me feel awful. I loved my husband. I probably still do.

That's why I keep going to meetings at the battered women's shelter and Al-Anon. I find the courage there not to look back, to hold fast to the hope I've moved on to, and to keep building my future.

Clarissa
age 29

Hung Up on Logistics

I was very hung up on a lot of logistics about what marriage should or shouldn't be, who should do what, how we should behave, how we should live.

When I got divorced, I lost all those structural expectations. When all those expectations were gone, I was able to see what was really missing from my relationship. I didn't need all those logistics to be married.

Now future relationships are free to take on lots of different forms. They are free to become whatever they need to be in my life without being constricted by irrelevant structural concepts that may not be appropriate to my relationship.

Drew
age 39

ATTENTION TO ME

I really lucked out with my stepmom. I was determined not to be nice to her. But she did some really cool things.

She always made sure I had time alone with my dad. She'd make the arrangements for us to go to a baseball game—just Dad and me. If I was staying with them, she'd always disappear for hours on end while Dad and I hung out at their apartment. Sometimes she'd leave us a chore to do together. It was always something Dad didn't know how to do, like cooking or hanging the curtain rods. She'd say, "I'm glad you're there to help your dad because this is not what he's best at." Dad called our chores "problem-solving teamwork." We messed up a lot, but it was always pretty funny.

She made it very clear that she wasn't my parent, that she wasn't going to replace my mom. And she always spoke well of my mom. Even when Dad was angry at Mom, she'd encourage Dad to calm down and at least see Mom's side of the story even if he didn't agree with it. That let me know I didn't have to take sides, which was a big relief.

Now I really like and trust her. I know she likes me, too. I know she pays attention to me, and it feels good to be needed.

Rosemary
age 13

REFLECTIONS

When I changed my life, when I stopped running away and focused on my home life and my children, I also made a courageous compromise: I would stay in Boston despite my dream of moving west.

I had lived from age seven to twenty-four in Italy; Boston, with its post-Puritan heritage and controlled intellectual and cultural expectations, felt repressive and stifling to me. And I longed to escape the shadow of my ex-husband's political career.

But there were good reasons for staying put. I had wonderful, caring friends. And I had children in school.

I was not willing to remove my children from their support system. I needed the continuity and support as much as they did. Equally important was the children's need to be near their father when he came back to Boston from Washington, D.C., on weekends. If I moved away, they would rarely have time with him. So I resigned myself to staying in Boston until my youngest graduated from high school. That meant I would have to wait thirteen years until I could act on my dream of moving west.

Julia

Taking Responsibility

I now know that divorce is a process. Each step to divorcing has a purpose. And most of the steps are emotional ones.

I went up and down a lot of steps before I could truly move on with my life, no matter how resolved I looked to the outside world. I had to overcome fear to be able to leave my marriage. I had to realize that moving to another town was not a solution. I had to recognize and bear the grief I felt when my ex-husband remarried.

The process taught me valuable lessons. Probably the most valuable was that I needed to take responsibility for what I didn't have in my first marriage. So, after I had grieved my ex-husband's remarriage, I sat down and wrote a list of everything I wanted if I ever remarried.

I based the list on who I was as a person—my good and my bad traits. For example, I admitted I was a "care-taker"—I catered to other people's needs before my own—so I needed to be with a man who was exceptionally kind and sensitive, even if he didn't fit the popular silent, strong image of maleness.

I compromised with a couple of men I dated. But soon all those uncomfortable feelings came back—that sort of draining feeling when you give away more of yourself than you get back from the relationship.

Finally, I refused to compromise. I waited several years. But it was worth it. I have an incredible second marriage.

Leonora
age 34

LIBERATION

Most of the men I know who have been divorced only pretend they have their lives together. For a while, my way of coping was to go to the bar, work too hard, play some intense game like football, or get angry and domineering. I thought it worked because I was able to numb my feelings.

The feelings kept coming up again and again, though. I kept getting into new relationships that wouldn't last. Every time they came apart I had to reexperience all the crud of my divorce.

I was always complaining about being broke because I had to pay my wife alimony.

Finally I stopped having everyone and everything be responsible for my state of mind. I stopped being a victim. I got my act together. I tightened my belt. I focused on my needs and set goals for myself.

I feel pretty good about myself now. I was putting a lot of energy into being confrontational and feeling sorry for myself. I'm using that energy now to build my future. It feels really liberating.

Bradley
age 37

ENDING THE LEGAL BATTLE

I finally let go of fighting. What I needed was some good therapy so that I could heal the self-esteem wounds and feelings of loss I was suffering from when my husband left me so suddenly for the young coanchor who does the news with him.

I now know he left not because I did something wrong but because he needed something for himself. Fighting with him, working with a lawyer who used scorched-earth tactics to grind him into the ground, wasn't going to ease my feelings of rejection. The legal fight was harsh, abusive, and expensive and was hurting me, too.

I now have a new lawyer who has helped me set legal and financial standards that will keep me economically safe and that the judge will accept. After all, in the end, no matter what state you live in, it's the judge who decides what is or isn't fair in a divorce. Trying to go for blood, to call my ex names and accuse him in court, which is what I would have to do to gouge him for everything he's got, is a waste of my time and money and not a way I want to think of myself as behaving.

There is no question that he doesn't want to pay me my due. He wants to have as much as possible to indulge himself and his new lifestyle. But there are laws and legal precedents that protect my interests. The best thing I can do for myself is know what those laws and legal precedents are so that I can be sure my lawyer is doing everything he should to protect my rights.

I want to move on. Ending the legal battle is only part of it. I've also ended his existence in my house. I've redecorated his office and turned it into a pretty library. There's no longer a TV in it, and I no longer torture myself by watching the two of them on the news. I'm doing everything I can to move on to a new life.

Rachael
age 50

A Peaceful Compromise

It is not easy being a stepparent. Your stepkids are pre-pared and ready to mistrust you. It takes patience and compromise to get over the initial adjustment. I think I got the most positive results from making sure that I respected them for who they were and that they respected me for who I was. We were definitely different stripes of cat. As long as I didn't try to change them or "get in their face," as they like to say, then we had a peaceful compro-mise.

We all—their dad, the kids, and I—sat down and went over the ground rules for our new household. Everybody got to participate and include a rule that was sacred to them. We wrote them down on a piece of paper and posted it on the refrigerator. I think that exercise made the kids feel part of a whole rather than people who were fit-ting in to their father's and my new life.

To be honest, there were times when I wanted to scream at them. They had different habits that drove me a little nuts in the beginning. But I realized if I picked on all their habits, especially the habits they got away with in their mother's house, it would be tantamount to picking on their mother, and that's a sure way to alienate a stepchild. Also, you don't build cooperation by being critical, unilateral, or domineering.

Anne
age 37

EXPANDING

It requires expanding to move on to a relationship with a man other than your child's father. It's like building a third bay onto your two-car garage. The third car—your child's father—may not always be in the extra space, but you have to leave the room for it so that it doesn't break anything when it needs to fit in.

When I figured that out, I stopped feeling conflicted and confused. I was able to sort out my relationships. I began to consider my ex as another member of my extended family. Like a brother or something similar, he was someone to whom I had lifetime ties; there would always be an ongoing dynamic. I didn't have to be intimate with him, but I did have to include him.

Eventually, instead of resenting him, I grew to accept him. And the man I'm now married to no longer feels threatened by my ex's role in my life.

Deidre
age 50

Kid Rank

I give all my friends whose parents are divorcing one piece of advice. When their parents start complaining about each other in front of them, they should say, "Mom or Dad, I'm pulling kid rank. I'm sorry you're upset. But you're upset about a relationship problem between the two of you. I'm your kid. It's not fair to put me in the middle of your relationship problem."

I did it to my parents. It stunned them a bit at first. But they heard me and left me alone. I got to have independent relationships with each parent without feeling I had secrets to keep.

Mina
age 19

REFLECTIONS

I've learned from my divorce. My mistakes have taught me a lot, even though I still wince when I think of some of the things I did as I struggled through the early years of separation. I have, over time, gained perspective on my own behavior and feelings. I have learned to forgive myself. I know myself better. I like myself better. And I certainly like the new life I have chosen for myself.

My divorce has also put perspective on my parents' divorce, helping to heal old wounds. I have been able to understand what might have triggered some of my parents' behaviors and why those behaviors affected me the way they did. Once I was angry and resentful; now I consider their fumbles with compassion.

Julia

DIVORCE TAUGHT ME

Divorce taught me how to turn my life around.

At the beginning of my divorce process, I couldn't bear all my feelings, so I drank a lot. A friend took me to an Alcoholics Anonymous program. There were other people in the program getting divorced, too.

It was a comfort knowing there were others out there going through what I was going through. It makes a big difference knowing that someone else is howling inside, too. You know you are not alone.

I learned to share my chaotic feelings, my pain. When I could share my feelings, my mind stopped chattering at a thousand miles an hour. I stopped blaming myself for what had happened to my marriage. I found some peace.

I got back into art. I had given up that part of me. I expressed a lot of what I was feeling through my art. Now I've changed jobs. I teach painting in a high school. Life is good.

Magda
age 48

STARTING OVER

I'm living with a man again. This is the first serious relationship I've had since my divorce twelve years ago. To be honest, I hadn't been on a date in six years before I met Mark. So I'd been celibate, too.

Terror! That's what I felt when I realized my relationship with Mark was getting serious. I was terrified of sex. I was older; I'd been through menopause; I didn't know if my body would work.

I was terrified of caring. I had learned how to be on my own. I had gotten used to being lonely. I didn't want to get used to having Mark in my life. What would happen if it didn't work out? I would have to go through all the pain of learning to live with loneliness again. I didn't want to have to go through all that loss.

And I didn't trust my judgment. I hadn't picked the best guys to go out with after my divorce. I was so needy that I always fell for the man who made even the littlest fuss over me. I was blinded by need. I could never see beyond the facade. Inevitably, they left me because I'd get so clingy. Every time I got left, it brought up the divorce. I blamed myself, so I stopped going on dates. By the time Mark came around, I was well defended and very independent.

Mark is a very kind man. We took our time. It was painful, sometimes, breaking through our defenses, learning to trust, exploring new frontiers of intimacy. But it was worth it. I've never been happier!

Rebecca
age 57

New Standards for Living

I actually am grateful for my parents' divorce. It set new standards for living.

My mom knew that her relationship with my dad wasn't a good one. She really wanted my brother, sister, and me to live in a healthy household—a household full of honesty and respect for each of us. Instead of trying to make the best of a bad situation, she left Dad.

We've had to make a lot of adjustments. I've been pretty angry sometimes and very confused. But ... I'm older now. I can see the huge difference between my mom's household and my dad's. It's very clear why they couldn't and shouldn't be married.

Watching each of them set standards for their new lives has taught me. In my mom's house, there's a new format for discussing and relating. Everything is very warm and real. In my dad's house, it's all the same as before—everything on his terms and timing regardless of our needs or personalities. I love Dad, I don't judge him. I'm just not happy to visit him too much. So, I've learned what is comfortable and right for me. It has taught me a lot about who I am and what I want for myself.

Valerie
age 23

Forgiving

You have to love yourself before you can love someone else. You have to be able to forgive yourself for your weaknesses and mistakes so you can forgive your partner for his weaknesses and mistakes. You can't love if you can't forgive.

Carol
age 57

Moving On

I've been married and divorced three times. I have three grown children who are stable and happily married. Each of my marriages lasted an average of fourteen years. I was eighteen the first time I married; I was sixty the last time I got divorced. When I was eighteen I wanted fur coats, silver, and a duplex apartment in New York City. Now I want to live in three sparsely furnished rooms on the edge of a mesa. My physical needs have changed; my emotional needs have changed. That's what life is about: change, movement, learning, curiosity, personal growth.

So when my marriages dissolved I never had a sense of failure. I knew I had done everything I could to try and "save" the relationship. The time had come to move on . . . or, in my case, on and on!

Katherine
age 62

REFLECTIONS

In August of 1991, I was introduced to a man who, I realized over the next year, met all the criteria on the list I had made five years earlier of what I wanted in a partner. I wasn't looking for him. He just appeared one day at the ranch I had visited almost every summer since my separation.

A year later my youngest daughter decided to go to boarding school. My oldest was already in college. Now I was alone in Boston where I had never been happy, halfway across the country from someone who was rapidly becoming the second great love of my life.

I agonized. Could I sell the house and move? If my children no longer lived at home, could I live by myself in a place where I had been so unhappy?

With the help of my women's group and other dear friends, I made the decision to move, one year short of my fiftieth birthday. After twenty-three years in Boston, eleven of them on my own, I started a new life and a new partnership in Wyoming.

To relocate to a small town far away from the shadow of my old sadness was to provide myself with a tremendous freedom and the opportunity to regain the rich, autonomous identity I had had before marriage. I had truly moved on.

Julia

Here I am, where I ought to be.

Isak Dinesen, *Out of Africa*

VI

FINDING GUIDANCE AND COUNSEL

Practical Words from

Professionals Who Care

PAIN AND COURAGE

When you work in the area of domestic law, you develop a great deal of respect for the pain experienced by divorcing couples and the courage they use to cope with that pain.

Lawyer

Empowering Clients

I don't think that the "best" lawyers are the most ruthless or expensive—the ones who go for the jugular or the big settlement. The "best" lawyers are those who empower their clients, not victimize them.

Divorce is primarily an emotional process. It's like a death in the family. As divorce lawyers, we need to acknowledge the anger and sorrow attached to the loss, not exploit it. If we can advise our clients on how to find help to move through the grieving stages, then we can find equitable settlements that leave the divorcing individuals with some dignity. Legal revenge, settlement gouging, and protracted court cases only create more loss and more victims.

Lawyer

Hard-Core Lawyers

There is a small minority, a small hard core of lawyers who, for whatever reason, determine that their reputation is enhanced by being known as bomb throwers or whatever.

Although I have noticed a national toning down of this antagonistic approach, law schools are not changing their curriculums.

Most law schools do not include techniques of negotiation. Law students are taught how to litigate. So when faced with domestic or matrimonial work, they approach the problem as if it were an antitrust case instead of a complicated issue charged with human emotions.

Lawyer

IF I HAVE TO GO TO COURT, I'VE FAILED

Divorce is expensive.

The amount of money spent on revenge is appalling. As a divorce lawyer, I believe that if I have to go to court with my client, I've failed. There's no such thing as a cozy, civilized trial.

Going to court usually means you are not going to have a decent relationship with your spouse. If you have children, that's even more devastating.

Going to court is expensive. The average person can't afford to spend two or three hundred dollars an hour for a lawyer to go out and play war games. Even if he or she can afford it, there are much better things to do with money than underwrite aggression.

Going to court is divisive and time-consuming. And for kids, a trial is almost a guarantee that their parents will never speak again.

Lawyer

INFORMED DECISIONS

Divorce is a process with five psychological stages—denial, depression, anger, letting go, and moving on. I believe the legal profession falls down because they try to negotiate a settlement during the "depression" stage.

Mediation is a process of making informed decisions to resolve conflict. To mediate properly, the client has to know what he or she wants. I tell people to go away if they're not ready and to come back when they know what they want.

The trouble is that lawyers often come in and take advantage of the indecision and emotional confusion. People who can't decide what they want generally go and get lawyers who, in turn, go for lots of money.

Mediation can't happen if one party is trying to dominate another or is being abusive. Divorces negotiated by lawyers tend to be confrontational, all about winning or losing. Divorces negotiated by mediators are about being equitable.

Once a divorce has been mediated, that's when lawyers are helpful. Lawyers can draw up the contract that's already been mediated.

Mediator

Marshaling the Forces

Sometimes a lawyer has to light the legal fire, start beating the legal drum, even though it's not really the thing that should be happening.

For example, a woman comes in to my office and she's still in love. She tells me she can't understand what she did wrong, can't understand why this marriage is ending, can't understand why he was in such a hurry to move out, and by the way, she hasn't gotten any money from the guy for six weeks.

I'm asking her if she brought a certified copy of her marriage certificate. I'm marshaling the forces, preparing a Complaint for Divorce and a Motion for Temporary Orders. I'm starting all the controversial parts of divorce, the legal procedures that protect and provide for her. She's sitting there sobbing.

I should be telling her to go see a therapist, that she's not ready for divorce. But how can I tell her that? She doesn't have enough money to put groceries on the table.

Lawyer

Accepting the Divorce

From my perspective, far too many of our clients are just unprepared to be divorced. They're not ready. They either haven't taken the time or haven't been accorded the opportunity to get ready to be divorced.

Being ready means both members of the couple have accepted that they are divorcing. They may regret it, but they know it is necessary. They know what they want from a divorce agreement.

When a new client comes into my office, I put a piece of paper in front of them that has a list of everything they have to talk about, starting with kids and going all the way through how they file their tax return. If I put that piece of paper down in front of them and they pick it up and look at it and say, "Oh, yeah, I've done this, I've thought about that, I've talked about this," then I know they're ready. But if they look away or frown, then I know they're probably not ready.

I find that much of the recidivism—you know, the whole routine of going repeatedly back to court, filing for contempts or modifications—is a direct result of the fact that the couple wasn't ready to begin with.

If a couple isn't ready, it costs a fortune and it causes so much pain. If a couple is ready, it's thrilling to be able to help them go forward in a positive way.

Former judge/current divorce lawyer

CONSENSUS

For a divorce to be constructive, readiness is everything.

If a divorcing couple comes into my office and one of them is sobbing and the other one's looking out the window, I say, "Are you in agreement about why you're here?" One of them will say "yes" and the other one will say "no." The task then is to bring them to a place where they are both reading from the same page, so to speak— which means that they have an understanding of what brought them to divorce and a consensus that the marriage is over.

To bring them to that place, they have to experience a lot of denial, anger, and bargaining. They will say things like, "Maybe if we did this or changed that, then maybe we could get back together again." But then they catch up with where they are emotionally and come to understand that they are going through a vital process of letting go. Eventually, they can forgive each other for the bad parts of their marriage and honor the really good parts.

That's when they're ready to get divorced without destroying each other. Most couples who are ready go to a mediator, if they haven't already, to make a property and custody settlement. The lawyer is just a support to write up the legal document.

Psychotherapist

VIOLENCE

There is very often violence around the time of divorce.

Parents and children who are exposed to domestic violence are the neediest. Special care is required during divorce proceedings.

There are several considerations. First, it is very hard to get a truthful answer from any party. The victimized individual has a hard time asking for their needs if they are afraid of having their head smashed in by their spouse.

For that reason, in many states, mediation is not allowed if there is evidence of domestic abuse. So the divorce process almost automatically escalates because there is no method to apply understanding, healing, or therapeutic practices.

When the process escalates, the child's needs often get overlooked. If a child has simply witnessed violence, that constitutes abuse. Conditions should be set for visitation so that that child is not alone with the violent parent. The child is at risk. Courts often only concentrate on the victim, overlooking the child's passive victimization.

We need to be very aware of all aspects of domestic violence. Counseling and protection should always be legally required.

Lawyer

TIME HELPS

By the time I get involved, the custody issue between two divorcing parents is at the worst stage. There are some things I know to be true, and I try to bring that knowledge to the parents.

Time works for parents going through divorce. Time usually helps the parents get calmer and stronger. A parent who is in crisis cannot make a clear decision about the welfare of their child. If they could, they wouldn't be in such disagreement that I need to be appointed to assess and advise on who should get custody. Over time the emotional charge fizzles somewhat, and some rational sense can be regained.

Parents need to try and work out the care of their child outside of court with third-party advisers who help them think rationally. If parents can't reach an agreement outside the court, then a total stranger, the judge, on the word of other total strangers—lawyers, guardians ad litem, witnesses—is going to make decisions for the welfare of a family they know nothing about.

Kids are not bank accounts. They are living, breathing, reactive, vulnerable, precious beings who cannot be pushed and pulled, signed over and delivered, analyzed, dissected, divided, or ripped apart because of the selfish possessive needs of parents. Kids do not need to sit in court and hear a steady escalation of accusations, most of which are often not true, because the parents cannot look beyond their personal power struggle.

Guardian ad litem
(Court-appointed advocate for children's rights)

FLEXIBLE, CONSISTENT, AND PATIENT

When parents ask me how to tell their children they are divorcing, I always tell them to reassure the child that they love them and that the child is not the reason the parents are divorcing. I tell them not to fight in front of the child, especially about money and custody. I tell them to set up extra time to be available. To be flexible and, above all, consistent and patient.

I tell them not to mislead the child by pretending the divorce is going to be great because their parents are going to be happier. The parents should tell the child the truth, using love and compassion. They should say, "It is going to be hard, but we are going to do the best we can to keep you from falling between the cracks." Then the parents should stick by their words.

Child counselor

MAKE IT OKAY FOR THE CHILD

Say, for example, the dad doesn't come to pick up the kid at the arranged time. He's late or he doesn't come at all. The mom, who may well have had plans to do something, is furious. She should not vent her anger at her ex-husband in front of the child. That will only compound the child's feelings of rejection. The child knows full well that his or her dad has not come to see them. The mother's anger will only make the child suffer more.

The parent has the power to make it okay for the child. The child cannot make it okay. He or she doesn't have the tools to understand or make choices to rectify what has happened. Rather than screaming in front of the child that the father is irresponsible or a deadbeat, the mom could say something like, "I'm sure something came up and your dad couldn't make it. I'll talk to him later and find out what happened. Let's you and I go find something special to do."

Of course, if the mom had something she was planning to do without her kid, this sudden situation presents her with a lot of disappointment. But divorce requires special adjustments for special circumstances if the kids are to make it through the readjustment of their family structure. Divorcing parents need to take responsibility for that no matter how mad they are at each other.

Later, when the kid is not around, the mother can scream her lungs out at the dad. But the kid does not need to hear it.

Guidance counselor

ACCEPTING FAILURE

As a psychiatrist, I think one does have to look at divorce as something of a failure—the failure of a relationship, not a personal failure. Unless you recognize to some degree that there was a mistake made, you won't avoid personal failure and shame in a divorce.

If a divorcing couple can accept that there has been a failure of relationship, then they can understand how not to make the same mistakes the next time. This understanding is especially important if the couple has children, because they will have to relate on so many issues while bringing up their children.

If they can accept that the relationship failed and not themselves, they will be able to relate to each other as parents from a healthier perspective. They will talk about each other in a more supportive way; they will conceptualize the failure of relationship for what it really was rather than blaming each other. This ability to relate without blaming will be much healthier for the children.

So I encourage couples to accept failure so that they are not afraid of it and can come to understand *what* has failed, not *who* has failed.

Psychiatrist

GRACEFULLY LEAVING THE MESS

I tell my clients to go to therapy—not necessarily to figure out how to fix the mess they are in but rather to learn how to get out of the mess in the best way possible and to figure out how to avoid a similar mess in the future.

I can tell them this because I can say, "I've been there. I've married. I've divorced. And now I'm married to the most wonderful man in the world. There is life after divorce. What you are going through is what lots of people are going through. You will act like a nut for a period of time. You are going to cry. You are going to be depressed. You are going to think you are in love with him when you're most likely not because you just don't want to be alone. Lots of people feel the same way. You are not an odd character whose situation is completely unlike anyone else's. You are going to behave no different than I did when I was divorcing."

When I tell them that, they feel better and it gives them hope. Therapy then seems like a helpful tool rather than a reason to think there's something wrong with them.

Lawyer

Change Can Lead to Happiness

One of the best "deals" I ever negotiated was for a fifty-year-old woman who was abruptly dumped by her husband, a powerful doctor, for his nurse. I call the woman "my model client."

The wife, who had had major depression on and off, was being successfully treated at the time. Somehow she was able to put the needs of her children first and to realize that her best shot at a good financial result was to move quickly and to be reasonable.

She was also able to believe me when I said she was better off without her domineering husband and that she would be happier in three years than she had been in a long time.

I said to her, again and again, that my experience tells me that a lot that is positive will come out of her situation. You will learn strengths, interests, and independence you never knew you had before and that you wouldn't have discovered if you had stayed in this oppressive, empty, dead relationship.

She went back to school and got a degree in psychology. Now she's counseling in a women's center. I was absolutely right. She is happier than she has ever been. She says her paycheck makes all the difference to her self-esteem.

I think this is a very important story, especially for older women, who really feel they have been "displaced" when they face a divorce. They can develop a separate identity. They can bounce back and find a new life for themselves.

Lawyer

A Message of Hope

I have been a divorce mediator for twelve years. As a mediator I try to make divorce a positive experience by resolving the conflicts and maintaining a message of hope. Divorce is an upheaval. But upheavals do end.

Mediator

VII

SEEKING HELP

A Short Guide to Resources and

Support Relating to Divorce

On the following pages I have included information that I hope will be helpful as you manage the journey through divorce.

It is important to remember that *divorce is a process*—a complicated and intense process. Divorce, as a major life stress, presents many challenges and the need to adapt repeatedly. Everyone—you, your spouse, your children, your family and friends—will experience a change in life circumstances and a range of different emotions.

Your experiences will differ in detail and degree, and each of you will experience divorce at your own pace. For one person, the process may take six months; for another, it may take six years.

If you have *children*, pay special attention to them. They are going through a divorce, too. Many of the feelings you have, they may also experience. And they will also have intense emotions of their own. They are not the reason you are divorcing, but they usually think they are and need extra reassurance.

Sometimes the stresses and emotions of divorce can be overwhelming. You or someone in your family may be depressed. *Depression* is common and nothing to be ashamed of. On pages 181–85 we have listed symptoms for adults and children. If you suspect that you or your children are depressed, please get help. Depression can be treated, but untreated it can be life threatening.

Please remember, *violent behavior and sexual abuse* are not acceptable under any circumstances, no matter how awful you feel during the divorce process. Starting on page 179, I have included information on violence and on ensuring your safety from violence.

WHAT YOU CAN DO TO HELP YOURSELF

• Remember that you are not alone and that you have a right to your feelings. Do not let anyone shame you.

• Find someone you trust and can talk to about your feelings. This may be a friend, a professional therapist, an adult member of your family, or a rabbi, minister, or priest. Whether they are a friend or a professional, please make sure that you trust and feel safe with them. Look for someone who is empathic and does not shame, criticize, or force you into any action you are not ready to take.

• Join a support group. People and places where you may find support include school counselors, counseling services available at work, health maintenance organizations (HMOs), your local minister or priest, and twelve-step programs such as AA. (See page 187 for resources.) If money is a problem, remember that twelve-step programs and your local church offer free services. Similar services may be available at your local hospital or mental health center.

• Engage yourself in an activity or hobby that you enjoy, or join a group that engages in an activity you enjoy, such as a book club, an outdoor group, or the YMCA.

• Consult a lawyer or mediator to find out what your rights are and if legal proceedings are appropriate. (See page 186 for resources.) Remember that lawyers and mediators work for you. You are paying them to protect and advise you. Tell them what you want. They are a resource for you to use, but they are not the people who lead the way.

• Get rest, eat properly, and exercise.

• Be kind, patient, and forgiving with yourself and your family.

VIOLENCE

Please remember: violent behavior and sexual abuse are not acceptable under any circumstances, no matter how awful you feel.

If you have thoughts of harming or killing yourself or anyone else, or if someone is harming or has threatened to harm you or your children, please call the police and seek professional help.

On page 194, we show you whom and where to call for help.

Listed here are some signals that may indicate whether you are at risk of violence and/or sexual abuse.

ARE YOU IN DANGER?

Sometimes the signals that you or people you care for are in danger are clear and obvious. At other times, because you are confused, in crisis, or depressed it is hard to determine whether your safety is threatened.

Always remember to take the time you need to figure out and pay attention to your feelings. If you have an intuition that your partner might hurt you or someone you care for, that feeling, whether clear or vague, is enough of a reason to protect yourself.

The following are some signals that may indicate you are in danger, adapted from Ann Jones and Susan Schechter's book *When Love Goes Wrong*.

Your safety may be at risk if:

- You have a feeling of danger.
- A person close to you is threatening to kill or hurt you, himself, other people or animals, or that person has a history of suicide and/or homicide attempts.
- A person close to you physically or sexually abuses a child.
- A person close to you attacks you physically or sexually.
- You seriously consider killing your partner or hiring someone to kill him or her for you, or you consider suicide as a way out of your situation.
- Threats, actual violence, or abuse from a person close to you becomes worse, bizarre, or reckless.
- A person close to you has weapons or has used weapons to threaten you or others.
- A person close to you attempts to control you or demonstrates extreme possessiveness by following you, checking up on you, accusing you of affairs, or limiting your activities.
- A person close to you has a history of drug and alcohol abuse or is currently abusing drugs and alcohol and he or she appears jealous, paranoid, controlling, or abusive.
- A person close to you is suspicious or afraid you may leave him or her and wants to stop you.
- A person close to you is afraid you will expose one of his or her secrets, such as any illegal activity you know about.
- A person close to you exhibits irrational behavior—such as hearing voices, imagining serious illness or loss, or having delusions of conspiracies against him or her.
- A person close to you claims not to remember his or her actions or refuses to admit that certain actions have occurred.

• A person close to you has been arrested for criminal activity but doesn't appear to care whether he or she is arrested again.

If you think you are in immediate danger, call 911 for police assistance. If you are not in immediate danger but think you could be at risk in the future, you will find places you can call for help and support on page 194.

DEPRESSION

Sometimes the feelings caused by divorce can be devastating in their intensity. You or your children may feel hopeless, unable to function or focus. You may be depressed. Depression is a common reaction to the emotional upheaval of divorce.

The symptoms of depression in adults are not the same as they are in children and adolescents. We list both sets of symptoms here.

If you or someone you love is depressed, remember that you are not alone. Please reach out to someone who can support you.

There are many people whom you already know who can help you. Friends, family members, and your doctor, priest, rabbi, or minister are a few examples.

There are many ways to find professional support and guidance. On page 187 we list organizations you can call for immediate support.

You can also use the telephone book. Look in the Yellow Pages under "D" for local depression support groups or in the government pages for "Mental Health Agencies."

It is important to seek help. While depression can be effectively treated, it can become life threatening if neglected.

If you or someone you love is feeling suicidal, is having death-related thoughts, feels like hurting himself or herself or hurting others, or if someone is hurting or has hurt you, please call one of the following:

- Call the operator: dial 0 and ask for a suicide hot line or tell the operator what has happened.
- Call the police: dial 911.
- Call a local hospital: ask for the emergency ward.

Signs of Depression in Adults

The following symptoms have been specified in the DSM-IV-R (*Diagnostic and Statistical Manual of Mental Disorders*), a guidebook used by therapists and other mental health professionals. Symptoms used in assessing depression in adults are not necessarily accurate when assessing depression in children and adolescents.

A person is likely to be depressed if five or more of the following symptoms have been present during the same two-week period and represent a change from previous behavior. At least one of the symptoms is either a depressed mood or a loss of interest or pleasure.

- The person is in a depressed mood most of the day, nearly every day.
- The person says he or she feels sad or empty, or cries easily or often.
- There is markedly diminished interest or pleasure in all or almost all activities most of the day, nearly every day.
- There is a significant change in weight, either a loss or gain, or a decrease or increase in appetite.
- The person develops sleep disturbances, having trouble either falling asleep or staying asleep, or sleeping too much.

• The person seems uncharacteristically agitated, exhibiting either excessive fidgeting or restlessness.

• The person is fatigued or shows loss of energy nearly every day.

• The person feels worthless or has excessive or inappropriate guilt nearly every day.

• The person has a diminished ability to think or concentrate or is indecisive nearly every day.

• The person has recurrent thoughts of death (not just fear of dying), mentions suicide or a plan for suicide, or makes a suicide attempt.

If you suspect depression in yourself or someone you love, it is important to get help.

Sometimes depression can be caused by a general medical condition or a reaction to medication. When you need to determine whether this is the case, a medical examination is recommended. A physician can also recommend a psychotherapist who can diagnose and treat depression. A trained psychotherapist is the appropriate person to assess the nature and severity of depressive illness.

Antidepressant medication may be prescribed. If so, please consult a licensed psychopharmacologist. The administration of antidepressant medication is a very precise science that should be practiced only by specialists.

Signs of Depression in Children and Adolescents

Divorce can be difficult for every member of the family. It is important to recognize and treat children and adolescents who become depressed. Depression can be successfully treated, but if neglected, it can become life threatening.

Depressed children and teenagers behave differently

than depressed adults. The American Academy of Child and Adolescent Psychiatry outlines the key symptoms of depression that parents need to be aware of:

- Persistent sadness
- No longer enjoys or looks forward to favorite activities
- Increased activity or irritability
- Frequent complaints of physical illness, such as headaches and stomachaches
- Frequent absences from school or poor performance in school
- Persistent boredom, low energy, poor concentration
- A major change in eating and/or sleeping patterns.

A depressed child who used to play often with friends may start spending a lot of time alone. Activities that were once fun may no longer bring joy. Depressed children and adolescents may say they want to be dead or may talk about suicide. They may abuse alcohol or other drugs.

It is possible that a child or adolescent who is causing trouble at home or at school may be depressed but that the parents and teachers don't recognize this. A child does not need to appear sad to be depressed.

Early diagnosis and medical treatment are essential for depressed children.

For help, parents can ask their physician to refer them to a child and adolescent psychiatrist who can diagnose and treat depression in children and teenagers. A child and adolescent psychiatrist is a physician with at least five years of additional training in child and adolescent psychiatry beyond regular medical school requirements. Psychologists and social workers who counsel families, children, and adolescents should also have special training.

As with adults, depression in children and adolescents can sometimes be caused by a general medical condition or a reaction to medication. A medical examination is required to determine whether this is the case. A medical doctor can also help you find a qualified psychotherapist who can help the child or adolescent with the emotional challenges of depression.

Antidepressant medication may be prescribed. If so, please consult a licensed psychopharmacologist. Administering antidepressant medication is a very precise science that should be practiced only by specialists.

RESOURCES

There are a number of organizations that can provide you with support at the local level. The organizations listed here are divided into categories to help you locate the type of support you may need. If you belong to an HMO, be sure to consider the resources that might be available to you through your health care program.

Not every organization may suit your needs. For each category, I've provided a list of questions to help you determine whether the services offered are right for you.

MEDIATION, LEGAL ADVICE AND SUPPORT

Questions to ask yourself: Do I want a mediator or a lawyer as I make decisions regarding my separation and divorce? How much money will each service cost me, and what can I afford? With what kind of a person do I work best? Is my mediator or lawyer someone I trust? (See section VI, "Finding Guidance and Counsel," p. 157.)

Academy of Family Mediators

The Academy of Family Mediators (AFM) provides referral lists of mediators within each state who are members of the academy. Family mediators can be used to help define the needs of each person involved in a divorce and can assist in reaching a consensus regarding settlements that satisfy all parties. Mediation is separate from therapy and is not a forum for emotional conflict.

500 South Highway 100, Suite 355
Golden Valley, MN 55416
(612) 525-8670

Association of Family and Conciliation Courts

This international organization promotes the development and improvement of court services for couples and their children. The AFCC provides publications and pamphlets about divorce issues and offers a resource directory of parent education programs throughout the United States. The directory is available for $20.50, which includes shipping and handling.

329 West Wilson Street
Madison, WI 53703
(608) 251-4001

SUPPORT AND COUNSELING

Questions to ask yourself: What are your emotional needs, and what are the emotional needs of your family? What type of support or counseling is available to you that meets your budget limitations? If you are currently involved with some type of therapy or support group, do you trust the person or people you are working with? Are you being shamed or told to do something you don't want to do? Are you depressed? (See "Depression," p. 181.)

American Association of Marriage and Family Therapists

This organization sends out a referral list of AAMFT-accredited marriage and family therapists. With the list comes a consumer guide that answers questions about the AAMFT.

1100 17th Street N.W., 10th Floor
Washington, D.C. 20005-2710
(202) 452-0109

American Psychiatric Association

The American Psychiatric Association is a professional organization for psychiatrists. Callers are referred to a branch office in their state. When they call the state office, they will then be referred to one or more practitioners in their own area or to a mental health center.

1400 K Street N.W.
Washington, D.C. 20005
(202) 682-6220

American Psychological Association

The American Psychological Association is a professional organization for psychologists. The national office refers callers to branch offices in each state. The state office takes the caller's name and phone number; then a referral coordinator returns the call and provides names of psychologists and mental health centers in the caller's area.

750 1st Street N.E., Suite 4000
Washington, D.C. 20002
(202) 336-5800

National Association of Social Workers

The National Association of Social Workers provides the names of social worker members in a caller's area.

750 1st Street N.E., Suite 700
Washington, D.C. 20002
(800) 638-8799

National Mental Health Association

The National Mental Health Association refers callers to a local affiliate chapter, which in turn helps the caller choose an appropriate therapist.

1021 Prince Street
Alexandria, VA 22314
(703) 684-7722

New Beginnings

This successful local organization offers a support group for people wishing to build a new life after marital separation or divorce. It has served as a model for others wishing to start similar groups.

13129 Clifton Road
Silver Spring, MD 20904-3247
(301) 384-0111

FAMILY AND PARENTING

Question to ask yourself: What are the needs of your family?

The Boston Parents' Paper

Although this newspaper is published in Boston, the paper's stories cover nationwide themes. Subjects include the challenges facing children, effective parenting, and resources for both parents and children. Subscriptions are available for $15 a year or $22 for two years.

P.O. Box 1777
Boston, MA 02130
(617) 522-1515

Center for the Family in Transition

This organization provides and evaluates educational programs, preventive information, clinical and mediation services, and training seminars.

5725 Paradise Drive, Building B, Suite 300
Corte Madera, CA 94925
(415) 924-5750
(415) 924-2976 (fax)

Children's Rights Council

The Children's Right's Council (CRC) is a ten-thousand-member organization providing literature, statistics, and support resources for families dealing with child-related divorce issues, such as custody, parenting, and making decisions in the best interests of the child. The CRC is affiliated with Parents Without Partners, Mothers Without Custody, and the Stepfamily Association of America.

220 I Street N.E.
Washington, D.C. 20002-4362
(202) 547-6227

The Double Dee: Divorce Dispatch for Kids

The *Double Dee* is a clever, action-oriented newsletter for children whose parents are in the process of, or are already, divorced. The newsletter also publishes comments sent in by readers. The subscription cost for twelve monthly newsletters is $24.

P.O. Box 547
Belmont, MA 02178
(617) 862-2737

Mothers Without Custody

For information about Mothers Without Custody and the services they provide, send a business-sized envelope along with two 32-cent stamps to P.O. Box 36, Woodstock, IL 60098.

P.O. Box 56762
Houston, TX 77256-6762
(800) 457-6962

Parents Without Partners

Parents Without Partners provides support-group meetings and social and recreational activities for parents who are separated or divorced, and it publishes *The Single Parent*. There are over five hundred chapters nationwide. The national office will send information about how to join a chapter in your area and will introduce you to a local contact person.

401 North Michigan Avenue
Chicago, IL 60614-4267
(800) 637-7974
(The office moved to Chicago one year ago. Office hours are 9:00 A.M. to 5:00 P.M. central daylight time.)

Single-Parent Resource Center

The Single-Parent Resource Center is a twenty-year-old organization that supplies single parents with information about child care, food, shelter, and legal counseling. The center can refer callers to support sources in their own communities.

141 West 28th Street, Suite 302
New York, NY 10001
(212) 947-0221

Stepfamily Association

This organization connects people dealing with stepfamily situations to support groups in their own area, and it publishes a newsletter that focuses on stepfamily issues.

215 Centennial Mall South, Suite 212
Lincoln, NE 68508
(402) 477-7837

Stepfamily Foundation, Inc.

Issues concerning stepparenting are the focus of this organization. The foundation tracks research, legal trends, statistics, and other information pertinent to stepfamilies, offers telephone counseling, and provides referrals to counselors throughout the country.

333 West End Avenue
New York, NY 10023
(212) 877-3244

SUBSTANCE ABUSE

Questions to ask yourself: Are you or someone you care about suffering from some form of substance abuse? How is the substance abuse affecting other members of your family, and what type of support do they need? As you check into the resources listed here, are you comfortable with their group dynamics? If you are concerned about your privacy, can you find organizations in nearby towns or neighborhoods that would provide help but offer greater anonymity?

Alcoholics Anonymous World Services

Alcoholics Anonymous (AA) is a voluntary, nonprofessional, twelve-step organization for people who wish to attain and maintain sobriety. Local meetings are held regularly and give members a chance to provide mutual support.

P.O. Box 459
Grand Central Station
New York, NY 10163
(212) 686-1100

Al-Anon, Al-Anon (ACOA), and Alateen

Al-Anon is a fellowship of relatives and friends of alcoholics. Al-Anon (ACOA) is part of Al-Anon and is for adult children of alcoholics. Alateen is also part of Al-Anon and is designed for younger relatives and friends of alcoholics. These groups all follow the twelve-step tradition and hold local support meetings. They are also helpful resources for individuals who are victims of violence and abuse and/or other dysfunctional relationship dynamics.

P.O. Box 862
Midtown Station
New York, NY 10018-0862
(800) 344-2666

DOMESTIC VIOLENCE

Questions to ask yourself: Are you or your family in immediate danger? See p. 179 for guidelines to see if you are at risk. Do you trust and feel safe among the people you are asking to help you?

The National Domestic Violence Toll-Free Hot Line
c/o Michigan Coalition Against Domestic Violence

Call toll free any time of day or night for information or referral to a support group or battered women's shelter anywhere in the United States.

P.O. Box 7032
Huntington Woods, MI 48070
(800) 333-7233
(800) 873-6363 TDD (number for the hearing impaired)

The National Coalition Against Domestic Violence

This national coalition works on behalf of battered women and provides statistics and resource information about domestic violence.

P.O. Box 15127
Washington, D.C. 20003-0127
(202) 638-6388

RECOMMENDED READING

Books can be a tremendous help, offering insight and information. The first four books listed here may be especially useful to you.

READ THESE, IF YOU READ NOTHING ELSE

The Good Divorce, by Constance Ahrons, Ph.D. (New York: HarperCollins, 1994). An upbeat, positive approach to successful divorce, which suggests that redefining family doesn't mean losing family. Highly recommended.

The Divorce Help Sourcebook, by Margorie L. Engel (Detroit: Visible Ink Press, 1994). An invaluable, easy-to-use, comprehensive resource and information guide about all aspects of divorce. Includes accurate and helpful advice on everything from lawyers to child care.

How to Survive the Loss of a Love, by Melba Colgrove, Harold H. Bloomfield, and Peter McWilliams (New York: Bantam Books, 1991). A small, comforting book on how to recover from a loss.

Crazy Time, by Abigail Trafford (New York: Harper & Row, 1982). An exceptional, accessible book offering vivid examples and advice about all phases of divorce.

GENERAL BOOKS ABOUT DIVORCE

Creative Divorce, by M. Krantzler (New York: Signet, 1973). A positive book, written in the mid-seventies but still pertinent today, which views divorce as a chance for personal growth and change.

Divorce and New Beginnings, by Genevieve Clapp, Ph.D. (New York: John Wiley & Sons, 1992). A book filled with useful information about all aspects of divorce and the process of rebuilding a life.

The Divorce Decisions Workbook, by Margorie L. Engel and Diana Gould (New York: McGraw-Hill, 1992). A comprehensive guide to the financial, legal, practical, and emotional aspects of divorce, including copies of forms you may encounter as you go through the divorce process.

Second Chances, by Judith Wallerstein and Sandra Blakeslee (New York: Ticknor & Fields, 1989). Loaded with statistics, this book presents research from the most comprehensive, long-term study ever done on divorce. The information can be alarming, and some scholars have questioned the research, but the authors still offer valuable insight into the divorce scenarios they found to be the most successful.

Life After Divorce, by Sharon Wegscheider-Cruse (Deerfield Beach, Fl.: Health Communications, 1994). While encouraging you to experience all your feelings and reactions, the author suggests ways to change the experience of divorce from tragedy to one of personal gain.

MEDIATION AND LEGAL ISSUES

The Divorce Decisions Workbook, by Margorie L. Engel and Diana Gould (New York: McGraw-Hill, 1992). While this is a comprehensive guide to all aspects of divorce, it is specifically helpful with financial and legal issues.

The Divorce Handbook, by James T. Friedman (New York: Random House, 1984). A thorough handbook that answers in detail all your questions about the legal aspects of divorce.

Getting Divorced Without Ruining Your Life, by Sam Margulies, Ph.D., J.D. (New York: Simon & Schuster, 1992). A practical guide based on real-life case studies, leading you through amicable litigation, negotiation, and mediation.

From Father's Property to Children's Rights, by Mary Ann Mason (New York: Columbia University Press, 1994). An analysis of child custody that seeks to clarify issues of children's and parents' rights.

Mediation Therapy, by J. M. Wiseman (Lexington, Mass.: D. C. Heath and Company, 1990). This book, written for mental health professionals, provides an interesting look at strategies for helping families in crisis make effective decisions.

The Responsible Parent, by C. Piper (New York: Harvester Wheatsheaf, 1993). A look at power, control, and parental responsibility in mediation.

FAMILY AND PARENTING

Families Apart, by Melinda Blau (New York: Putnam, 1993). A resourceful book with advice about maintaining a healthy family within the structure of divorce.

The Divorced Parent, by Stephanie Marston (New York: William Morrow and Company, 1994). An easy-to-read book offering practical advice and specific suggestions about how to raise well-adjusted children after divorce.

Helping Children Cope with Divorce, by Edward Teyber (New York: Lexington Books, 1994). A book covering the concerns of children during and after divorce and effective strategies parents can use in dealing with these concerns.

The Parents Book About Divorce, by R. Gårdner, M.D. (New York: Bantam Books, 1991). This book deals with the effect of divorce on the family and how to ease the transition for children whose parents divorce.

Mom's House, Dad's House, by Isolina Ricci, Ph.D. (New York: Collier Books, 1980). A practical guide to making joint custody effective.

My Kids Don't Live with Me Anymore, by Doreen Virtue (Minneapolis, Minn.: CompCare Publishers, 1988). A hopeful, helpful book for parents who lose custody of their children.

CHILDREN

Dinosaurs Divorce, by Laurene Krasny Brown and Marc Brown (Boston: Little, Brown, 1986). A picture book dealing with concepts and issues of divorce from a child's perspective through the experiences of a family of dinosaurs.

How It Feels When Parents Divorce, by Jill Krementz (New York: Alfred A. Knopf, 1992). Nineteen children between the ages of seven and sixteen tell about their family divorce experiences.

When Your Parents Get a Divorce, by Ann Banks, illustrated by Cathy Bobak (New York: Puffin Books, 1990). An interactive journal for children who are dealing with a divorce.

It's Not the End of the World, by Judy Blume (New York: Bantam Books, 1972). The narrator of this book is a seventh grader whose family is in the midst of a divorce. While the book is stereotypical in terms of male and female roles, it is an honest presentation of a teenager's viewpoint.

DOMESTIC VIOLENCE

The Courage to Heal, by Ellen Bass and Laura Davis (New York: HarperPerennial, 1992). A groundbreaking book for victims of childhood abuse.

Getting Free, by Ginny NiCarthy (Seattle: Seal Press, 1982). This book is extraordinarily helpful and accessible. It explores pertinent issues and suggests thoughtful activities designed to help people who are or have been in physically or emotionally abusive relationships.

When Love Goes Wrong, by Ann Jones and Susan Schechter (New York: HarperPerennial, 1987). A sympathetic, easy-to-read book that helps identify controlling partners, as well as ways to get out of the relationship.

SUPPORT AND COUNSELING

You Are Not Alone, by Julia Thorne (New York: HarperCollins, 1993). An empathic, hopeful, and easy-to-read book conveying the real experiences and coping skills of those suffering from depression.

Care of the Soul, by Thomas Moore (New York: HarperCollins, 1992). A powerful book that shows how spirituality and nurturing the soul add meaning to modern life.

The Depression Workbook, by Mary Ellen Copeland (Oakland, Calif.: New Harbinger Publications, 1992). A useful workbook for depression sufferers.

Forgiveness, by Robin Casarjian (New York: Bantam Books, 1992). A loving book that helps heal the past through forgiveness.

Full Catastrophe Living, by Jon Kabat-Zinn (New York: Delacorte Press, 1991). A practical, highly readable book on using the mind and body for emotional and physical well-being.

Overcoming Depression, by Demitri Papolos, M.S., and Janice Papolos (New York: HarperCollins, 1992). Provides up-to-date information on medical, scientific, and therapeutic aspects of depression. Its discussion of insurance coverage is particularly useful.

The Rag and Bone Shop of the Heart, edited by Robert Bly, James Hillman, and Michael Meade (New York: HarperCollins, 1995). An anthology of poems and commentaries for men, which deal with a variety of themes, including the landscapes of loving.

Rebuilding When Your Relationship Ends, by Dr. Bruce Fisher (San Luis Obispo, Calif.: Impact Publishers, 1992). This book is a helpful, detailed guide through the stages of grief, healing, and rebuilding for people who've ended a marriage or long-term love relationship.

Silencing the Self, by Dana Crowley Jack (Cambridge, Mass.: Harvard University Press, 1991). A pioneering theoretical discussion about women and depression.

The Stormy Search for the Self, by Christina Grof and Stanislav Grof (Los Angeles: Jeremy P. Tarcher, 1990). A fascinating discussion of how spiritual emergencies can be transformational.

Women, Sex, and Addiction, by C. D. Kasl (New York: Harper & Row, 1989). Kasl's exploration of sex and addiction is informative and engaging. The text is dense but worth the effort.

When Feeling Bad Is Good, by Ellen McGrath (New York: Henry Holt, 1992). An innovative program for women on how to transform "healthy" depression into growth and power.

RELATING TO YOURSELF AND TO OTHERS

Finding Joy: 101 Ways to Free Your Spirit and Dance with Life, by Charlotte Davis Kasl, Ph.D. (New York: HarperCollins, 1994). A lighthearted but spiritual guide to bringing perspective and balance to your life.

Soul Mates, by Thomas Moore (New York: HarperCollins, 1994). A book about relationship to self and others, emphasizing how enriched our lives become as we live through the difficulties we encounter in our pursuit of intimacy.

Journey of the Heart: Intimate Relationships and the Path of Love, by J. Welwood (New York: HarperPerennial, 1990). A life-changing, soulful book of spiritual discovery that views relationship difficulties as opportunities for growth.

Forgiveness, by Robin Casarjian (New York: Bantam Books, 1992). A loving book that helps heal the past through forgiveness.

Getting the Love You Want: A Guide for Couples, by Harville Hendrix, Ph.D. (New York: HarperPerennial, 1988). A positive approach to transforming troubled intimate relationships into passionate friendships.

Rebuilding: When Your Relationship Ends, by Bruce Fisher, M.D. (San Luis Obispo, Calif.: Impact Publishers, 1981). A forthright book that takes you through the stages of recovery after ending a relationship and lists the steps toward building new relationships.

He: Understanding Masculine Psychology, by R. Johnson (San Francisco: HarperSanFrancisco, 1983). A book for both men and women, about the masculine psyche.

She: Understanding Feminine Psychology, by R. Johnson (San Francisco: HarperSanFrancisco, 1983). This book is the counterpart to *He* and explores the female psyche.

We: Understanding the Psychology of Romantic Love, by R. Johnson (San Francisco: HarperSanFrancisco, 1983). A book about the essence and meaning of romantic love.

ACKNOWLEDGMENTS

Like divorce, writing a book is a process that offers good moments and bad moments, frustrations, accomplishments, anger, and joy. I could not have negotiated the process without the support and skill of my assistant, Jean Weiss. Jean has many gifts: brilliance, focus, patience, dedication, humor, beauty, voice. She wears many hats: writer, magazine editor, mountain climber, hiking guide, rock-and-roll singer, dog walker, friend. She is also a child of divorce, so this is her book, too.

Jean and I spent long days honing the text. These days were made bearable by the location of my office: a large airy space surrounded by ponds, meadows, and trees. I will be forever grateful to Emily Stevens, who not only contributed the space attached to her ranch house but also made herself available for a chat, walk, or meal whenever I needed support.

Janet Goldstein, my original editor at HarperCollins, and Kris Dahl, my agent at International Creative Management, are the book's midwives. They took me to lunch and delivered divorce. I am grateful for their perseverance and vision. Janet's excellent vision includes her passing the reins to Hugh van Dusen, who kindly and ably stepped in as editor when she left for Broadway Books during the book's final edits.

Divorce has heroes; so does this book. I want to thank especially all the individuals who took the time to participate in a focus group or to be interviewed. They are too many to be mentioned individually, but I hope they know that there would not be a book without their courage and honesty and that I am truly grateful for their participation.

Gene Dahmen, divorce lawyer extraordinaire, is a special hero. On spring vacation with our families, Gene and I spent every morning under a beach umbrella resequencing the text. Gene is also responsible for putting me in touch with a remarkable team of professionals who are trying to change the antagonistic, opportunistic face of divorce. I wish every person experiencing divorce could benefit from the wisdom and expertise of my generous friend Gene.

Lynn Madsen and Denise Wilder, two talented psychologists, need recognition. Lynn is doing compassionate and insightful work on women and parenting. Denise has written a poignant brochure on divorce.

Steve Ashley, the owner of Valley Bookstore, is a hero who contributed a bookcase-full of resource and research material.

Diggity deserves special thanks for spending so many hours in my office.

Margo Howard is an unending source of information and inspiration. So are Louis Borgenicht, Belton Copp, Evie Frost, and Nancy Meyers Coolidge who all took the time to read and make suggestions on the text.

Throughout this book I encourage building a network of support because I couldn't have managed the lengthy journey of my own divorce without the guidance and support of my friends, especially Diane DiCarlo and Gail Marcus. Fearless in their pursuit of truth, they carried the torch for my best interests whenever I faltered. And then there is the special category labeled "Anne and John Milliken," two friends who read, argued, hugged, fed, and, whenever I doubted, let me know in no uncertain terms the nature of their relationship to me: "Unconditional love, babe!"

Unconditional love for Alexandra, Vanessa, and Rich, too.